# ELE
# PO

**K**

## SEVENTH EDITION – 1993

UPDATED TO 1994 EDITION 1.1.94

The Complete Guide to all
BR Electric Multiple Units

Peter Fox

ISBN 1 872524 48 6

Pocket

# CONTENTS

# FROM THE PUBLISHER

Platform 5 Publishing are still the only company to provide the enthusiast or transport official with complete information on BR rolling stock. This book is updated to 5th December 1992 and is, at the time of publication, the most up-to-date publication of its type on the market.

This book also contains details of the stock of Eurotunnel.

# NUMBERING

BR design electric multiple unit vehicles are numbered in the series 61000 – 78999. SR vehicles carry numbers in the SR 14000 – 15999 number series, and there is one unit kept for special duties with vehicles numbered in the LNER 6xxxx number series. Isle of Wight and Waterloo & City line vehicles are numbered in a separate series.

Regional prefix letters used to be carried preceeding the vehicle number, but these are now no longer used and many have been removed. The prefixes were: E – Eastern Region, M – London Midland Region, S – Southern Region, SC – Scottish Region. Prefixes are not shown in this book as they no longer officially form part of the vehicle number. In addition, SR number series vehicles used to carry the suffix S.

In this book, stock is generally listed in order of the unit or set number. The set number is stated first, followed by any notes applicable to the particular set. These are followed by codes for livery, sector and depot respectively. Finally the numbers of the individual cars in the set are given, in order. Please note that reformations can and do occur.

# NOTES

Unless stated otherwise, all multiple unit vehicles are of BR design, or designed by contractors for BR and have buckeye couplings and tread brakes. Seating is $3+2$ in standard class open vehicles, $2+2$ in first class open vehicles, 12 to a non-corridor standard class compartment, 8 to a corridor standard class compartment and 6 to a corridor first class compartment. In express stock, open standards have $2+2$ seating and open firsts have $2+1$ seating.

# ABBREVIATIONS

The following abbreviations are used in this book:

**Operator Codes:**

Each vehicle is referred to by an operator code as follows:

| | |
|---|---|
| M | Motor |
| DM | Driving Motor |
| BDM | Battery Driving Motor |
| T | Trailer |
| DT | Driving Trailer |
| BDT | Battery Driving Trailer |
| B | Brake, i.e. vehicle with luggage space and guards compartment. |
| F | First |
| S | Standard |
| C | Composite |
| U | Unclassified |
| RB | Buffet Car |
| H | handbrake fitted. |
| RSM | Buffet Standard (Modular) |
| PMV | Parcels and Mails Van |
| LV | Luggage Van |
| O | Open vehicle |
| K | Side corridor with lavatory |
| so | Semi-open vehicle. |
| L | Open or semi-open Vehicle with lavatory |
| MLS | Motor Luggage Standard (an MBS minus the guards equipment) |

The letters (A) and (B) may be added to the above codes to differentiate between two cars of the same operating type which have differences between them. Note that a consistent system is used, rather than the official operator codes which are sometimes inconsistent.

Notes:

(1) Compartment Stock (non-corrridor) has no suffix.
(2) Semi-open composites generally have the first class accommodation in compartments and the standard class in open saloons.
(3) Unless stated otherwise, it is assumed that motor vehicles are fitted with pantographs. If the pantograph is on a trailer, then the trailer has the prefix 'P', e.g. PTSO — Pantograph trailer open standard.

## GENERAL INFORMATION

### Builder Codes:

| | |
|---|---|
| ABB | ABB Transportation Ltd. |
| AEI | Associated Electrical Industries Ltd. |
| BRCW | The Birmingham Railway Carriage & Wagon Co. Ltd. |
| BTH | The British Thomson Houston Co. Ltd. |
| CP | Crompton-Parkinson Ltd. |
| EE | The English Electric Co. Ltd. |
| GEC | The General Electric Company Ltd. |
| Gloucester | The Gloucester Railway Carriage and Wagon Co. Ltd. |
| Hunslet | Hunslet Transportation Projects Ltd. |
| Metro-Cammell | The Metropolitan Cammell Railway Carriage and Wagon Co. Ltd. |

### Other Abbreviations:

| | |
|---|---|
| (S) | Stored Serviceable |
| (U) | Stored Unserviceable |
| LNER | London & North Eastern Railway |
| SR | Southern Railway |

## DIAGRAMS AND DESIGN CODES

For each type of vehicle, the official design code consists of a seven character code of two letters, four numbers and another letter, e.g. EC2040B. The first five characters of this are the diagram code and are given in the class heading or sub heading. These are explained as follows:

### 1st Letter

This is always 'E' for an electric multiple unit vehicle.

### 2nd Letter

as follows for various vehicle types:

| | |
|---|---|
| A | Driving motor passenger vehicles. |
| B | Driving motor passenger vehicles with a brake compartment. |
| C | Non-Driving motor passenger vehicles. |
| D | Non-Driving trailer passenger vehicles with a brake compartment. |
| E | Driving Trailer passenger vehicles. |
| F | Battery Driving Trailer passenger vehicles. |
| G | Driving Trailer passenger vehicles with a brake compartment. |
| H | Trailer passenger vehicles. |
| I | Battery Driving Motor passenger vehicles. |
| J | Trailer passenger vehicles with a brake compartment. |
| N | Trailer passenger vehicles with a buffet compartment. |
| O | Battery Driving Trailer passenger vehicles with a brake compartment. |
| P | Trailer passenger vehicles with a handbrake. |
| X | Driving Motor Luggage Vans. |
| Y | Non-driving Motor Luggage Van. |

### 1st Figure

| | |
|---|---|
| 1 | First class accommodation. |
| 2 | Standard class accommodation (incl. declassified seats). |
| 3 | Composite accommodation. |
| 5 | No passenger accommodation. |

# 25 kV a.c. OVERHEAD EMUs.

Note: All units are 25 kV overhead only except where stated otherwise.

## CLASS 302

BDTCOL – MBSO – TSOL – DTSO or BDTCOL – MBSO – DTSO. All remaining units refurbished with new seats, fluorescent lighting and pa.
**Gangways:** Within unit.
**Traction Motors:** Four EE536A 143.5 kW.
**Dimensions:** 19.50 x 2.82 m (outer cars), 19.36 x 2.82 m (inner cars).
**Maximum Speed:** 75 mph.

**75084 – 75205. BDTCOL.** Lot No. 30436. York/Doncaster 1958 – 59. Dia. EF303. 24F 52S 1L. 39.5 t. B5 bogies.
**75311 – 75358. BDTCOL.** Lot No. 30440. York/Doncaster 1959. Dia. EF303. 24F 52S 1L. 39.5 t. B5 bogies.
**61060 – 61091. MBSO.** Lot No. 30434. York 1958 – 59. Dia. ED216. 76S. 55.3 t. Gresley Bogies.
**61122 – 61226. MBSO.** Lot No. 30438. York 1960. Dia. ED216. 76S. 55.3 t. Gresley Bogies.
**70060 – 70091. TSOL.** Lot No. 30437. York/Doncaster 1958 – 59. Dia. EH223. 86S 1L. 34.4 t. B4 bogies.
**70122 – 70226. TSOL.** Lot No. 30441. York 1959 – 61. Dia. EH223. 86S 1L. 34.4 t. B4 bogies.
**75033 – 75079. DTSO.** Lot No. 30435. York 1958 – 59. Dia. EE219. 88S. 33.4 t. B4 or B5 bogies.
**75236 – 75283. DTSO.** Lot No. 30439. York 1959 – 60. Dia. EE219. 88S. 33.4 t. B4 or B5 bogies.

| | | | | | | | |
|---|---|---|---|---|---|---|---|
| 302 201 | | N | NTSX | EM | 75085 | 61060 | 70060 | 75033 |
| 302 202 | | | NTSX | EM | 75086 | 61061 | 70061 | 75034 |
| 302 203 | (302 263) | | NTSX | EM | 75311 | 61122 | 70122 | 75236 |
| 302 204 | | | NTSX | EM | 75088 | 61063 | 70063 | 75036 |
| 302 205 | | N | NTSX | EM | 75089 | 61064 | 70064 | 75037 |
| 302 207 | (302 310) | | NNEX | EM | 75358 | 61226 | 70226 | 75283 |
| 302 209 | | N | NTSX | EM | 75093 | 61068 | 70068 | 75041 |
| 302 210 | | | NTSX | EM | 75094 | 61069 | 70069 | 75042 |
| 302 211 | | | NTSX | EM | 75095 | 61070 | 70070 | 75043 |
| 302 212 | | | NTSX | EM | 75096 | 61071 | 70071 | 75044 |
| 302 213 | | | NTSX | EM | 75097 | 61072 | 70072 | 75060 |
| 302 214 | (302 304) | N | NTSX | EM | 75352 | 61220 | 70220 | 75277 |
| 302 215 | | | NNEX | EM | 75099 | 61074 | | 75062 |
| 302 216 | | N | NNEX | EM | 75100 | 61075 | | 75063 |
| 302 218 | | | NNEX | EM | 75191 | 61077 | | 75065 |
| 302 219 | | | NNEX | EM | 75192 | 61078 | | 75066 |
| 302 221 | | | NNEX | EM | 75194 | 61080 | | 75068 |
| 302 223 | (302 293) | | NNEX | EM | 75341 | 61209 | | 75266 |
| 302 224 | | N | NNEX | EM | 75197 | 61083 | | 75071 |
| 302 225 | | | NNEX | EM | 75198 | 61084 | | 75072 |
| 302 227 | (302 277) | N | NTSX | EM | 75325 | 61193 | 70193 | 75250 |
| 302 228 | | | NNEX | EM | 75201 | 61087 | | 75075 |

| | | | | | | |
|---|---|---|---|---|---|---|
| 302 229 | | NNEX | EM | 75202 61088 | | 75076 |
| 302 230 | (302 232) | NTSX | EM | 75205 61091 | 70091 | 75079 |

**Class 302/9. Parcels Units.** BDTPMV – MPMV – DTPMV.

**68100/3. BDTPMV.** Dia. EF501. Lot No. 30435. York 1959.
**68101 – 2. BDTPMV.** Dia. EF501. Lot No. 30439. York 1959.
**68020 – 1. MPMV.** Dia. ED501. Lot No. 30434. York 1959.
**68022 – 3. MPMV.** Dia. ED501. Lot No. 30438. York 1960.
**68207/10. DTPMV.** Dia. EE501. Lot No. 30435. York 1959.
**68208 – 9. DTPMV.** Dia. EE501. Lot No. 30439. York 1959.

| | | | | | |
|---|---|---|---|---|---|
| 302 990 | R | RPMA | IL | 68100 68020 68207 |
| 302 991 | R | RPMA | IL | 68101 68021 68208 |
| 302 992 | R | RPMA | IL | 68102 68022 68209 |
| 302 993 | R | RPMA | IL | 68103 68023 68210 |

Former numbers of converted vehicles:

| | | | | | |
|---|---|---|---|---|---|
| 68020 (61090) | 68023 (61222) | 68102 (75218) | 68208 (75217) |
| 68021 (61067) | 68100 (75084) | 68103 (75078) | 68209 (75219) |
| 68022 (61227) | 68101 (75221) | 68207 (75082) | 68210 (75074) |

**Spare MBSO/TSOL:**

| | | | | | | | |
|---|---|---|---|---|---|---|---|
| 61065 | 61079 | 61085 | 70075 | 70078 | 70083 | 70087 | 70209 |
| 61076 | 61081 | 70074 | 70077 | 70080 | 70084 | 70088 | |

# CLASS 303

DTSO – MBSO – BDTSO. Sliding doors.
**Bogies:** Gresley.
**Gangways:** None Gangwayed within units only (r).
**Traction Motors:** Four MV 155 kW.
**Dimensions:** 19.50 x 2.82 m (outer cars), 19.36 x 2.82 m (inner cars).
**Maximum Speed:** 75 mph.

**Class 303/0.** Unrefurbished sets.

**DTSO.** Dia. EE206. 83S. 34.4 t.
**MBSO.** Dia. ED201. 70S. 56.4 t.
**BDTSO.** Dia. EF202. 83S. 38.4 t.

**Class 303/1.** Refurbished with 2 + 2 seating and hopper-type window vents).
Denoted by 'r'

**DTSO.** Dia. EE241. 56S. 34.4 t.
**MBSO.** Dia. ED220. 48S. 56.4 t.
**BDTSO.** Dia. EF217. 56S. 38.4 t.

**75566 – 75599. DTSO.** Lot No. 30579 Pressed Steel 1959 – 60.
**75747 – 75801. DTSO.** Lot No. 30629 Pressed Steel 1960 – 61.
**61481 – 61514. MBSO.** Lot No. 30580 Pressed Steel 1959 – 60.
**61813 – 61867. MBSO.** Lot No. 30630 Pressed Steel 1960 – 61.
**75601 – 75634. BDTSO.** Lot No. 30581 Pressed Steel 1959 – 60.
**75803 – 75857. BDTSO.** Lot No. 30631 Pressed Steel 1960 – 61.

| | | | | | | | |
|---|---|---|---|---|---|---|---|
| 303 001 | r | S | RAGW | GW | 75566 | 61481 | 75601 |
| 303 003 | r | S | RAGW | GW | 75568 | 61483 | 75603 |
| 303 004 | r | S | RAGW | GW | 75569 | 61484 | 75604 |
| 303 006 | r | S | RAGW | GW | 75571 | 61486 | 75606 |
| 303 008 | r | S | RAGW | GW | 75573 | 61488 | 75608 |
| 303 009 | r | S | RAGW | GW | 75574 | 61489 | 75609 |
| 303 010 | r | S | RAGW | GW | 75575 | 61490 | 75610 |
| 303 011 | r | S | RAGW | GW | 75576 | 61491 | 75611 |
| 303 012 | r | S | RAGW | GW | 75577 | 61492 | 75612 |
| 303 013 | r | S | RAGW | GW | 75578 | 61493 | 75613 |
| 303 014 | r | S | RAGW | GW | 75579 | 61494 | 75614 |
| 303 016 | r | S | RAGW | GW | 75581 | 61496 | 75616 |
| 303 019 | r | S | RAGW | GW | 75584 | 61499 | 75619 |
| 303 020 | r | S | RAGW | GW | 75585 | 61500 | 75620 |
| 303 021 | r | S | RAGW | GW | 75586 | 61501 | 75621 |
| 303 023 | r | S | RAGW | GW | 75588 | 61503 | 75623 |
| 303 024 | r | S | RAGW | GW | 75589 | 61504 | 75624 |
| 303 025 | r | S | RAGW | GW | 75590 | 61505 | 75625 |
| 303 027 | r | S | RAGW | GW | 75592 | 61507 | 75627 |
| 303 028 | r | S | RAGW | GW | 75600 | 61508 | 75635 |
| 303 032 | r | S | RAGW | GW | 75597 | 61512 | 75632 |
| 303 034 | r | S | RAGW | GW | 75599 | 61514 | 75634 |
| 303 035 | r | S | RAGW | GW | 75595 | 61860 | 75817 |
| 303 037 | r | S | RAGW | GW | 75773 | 61813 | 75803 |
| 303 038 | r | S | RAGW | GW | 75748 | 61814 | 75804 |
| 303 040 | r | S | RAGW | GW | 75750 | 61816 | 75806 |
| 303 043 | r | S | RAGW | GW | 75572 | 61819 | 75809 |
| 303 045 | r | S | RAGW | GW | 75755 | 61821 | 75811 |
| 303 046 | r | S | RAGW | GW | 75756 | 61822 | 75812 |
| 303 047 | r | S | RAGW | GW | 75757 | 61823 | 75813 |
| 303 048 | | 0 | RAGW | GW | 75752 | 61824 | 75808 |
| 303 054 | r | S | RAGW | GW | 75764 | 61830 | 75820 |
| 303 055 | r | S | RAGW | GW | 75765 | 61831 | 75821 |
| 303 056 | r | S | RAGW | GW | 75766 | 61832 | 75822 |
| 303 058 | r | S | RAGW | GW | 75768 | 61834 | 75824 |
| 303 060 | | G | RFXX | GW (U) | 75770 | 61836 | 75826 |
| 303 061 | r | S | RAGW | GW | 75771 | 61837 | 75827 |
| 303 065 | r | S | RAGW | GW | 75775 | 61841 | 75831 |
| 303 070 | r | S | RAGW | GW | 75780 | 61846 | 75836 |
| 303 073 | r | S | RAGW | GW | 75783 | 61849 | 75839 |
| 303 077 | r | S | RAGW | GW | 75787 | 61853 | 75843 |
| 303 079 | r | S | RAGW | GW | 75789 | 61855 | 75845 |
| 303 080 | r | S | RAGW | GW | 75790 | 61856 | 75846 |
| 303 082 | | G | RFXX | GW | 75792 | 61858 | 75848 |
| 303 083 | r | S | RAGW | GW | 75793 | 61859 | 75849 |
| 303 085 | r | S | RAGW | GW | 75795 | 61861 | 75851 |
| 303 087 | r | S | RAGW | GW | 75797 | 61863 | 75853 |
| 303 088 | r | S | RAGW | GW | 75798 | 61864 | 75854 |
| 303 089 | r | S | RAGW | GW | 75799 | 61865 | 75855 |
| 303 090 | r | S | RAGW | GW | 75800 | 61866 | 75856 |
| 303 091 | r | S | RAGW | GW | 75801 | 61867 | 75857 |
| Spare | | G | RFXX | GW (U) | 75773 | | 75829 |

| Spare | **S** | RFXX | GW (U) | 75785 | 75841 |
|-------|-------|------|--------|-------|-------|

# CLASS 304

BDTSOL – MBSO – DTBSO. Originally 4 cars.
**Bogies:** Gresley.
**Gangways:** None.
**Traction Motors:** Four BTH 155 kW.
**Maximum Speed:** 75 mph.
**Dimensions:** 19.53 x 2.82 m (outer cars), 19.36 x 2.82 m (inner cars).

**Class 304/1.** These cars have pairs of narrow windows instead of wide windows and the MBSOs were formerly MBS and were refurbished with new seats etc.

**BDTSOL.** Dia. EF203. Lot No. 30429 Wolverton 1960. 80S 2L. 36.8 t.
**MBSO.** Dia. ED215. Lot No. 30428 Wolverton 1960. 72S. 54.5 t.
**DTBSO.** Dia. EG202. Lot No. 30430 Wolverton 1960. 82S. 32.5 t.

| 304 002 | RCLG | LG | 75046 61046 75646 |
|---------|------|----|-----|
| 304 003 | RCLG | LG | 75047 61047 75647 |
| 304 004 | RCLG | LG | 75048 61048 75648 |
| 304 005 | RCLG | LG | 75049 61049 75649 |
| 304 006 | RCLG | LG | 75050 61050 75650 |
| 304 008 | RCLG | LG | 75052 61052 75652 |
| 304 009 | RCLG | LG | 75053 61053 75653 |
| 304 010 | RCLG | LG | 75054 61054 75654 |
| 304 013 | RCLG | LG | 75057 61057 75657 |
| 304 014 | RCLG | LG | 75058 61058 75658 |
| 304 015 | RCLG | LG | 75059 61059 75659 |

**Class 304/2.** Standard design with wide windows.

**75681 – 75698. BDTSOL.** Dia. EF204. Lot No. 30610 Wolverton 1960 – 61. 80S 2L. 36.8 t.
**75868 – 75875. BDTSOL.** Dia. EF204. Lot No. 30645 Wolverton 1961. 80S 2L. 36.8 t.
**61629 – 61646. MBSO.** Dia. ED203. Lot No. 30607 Wolverton 1960 – 61. 72S. 54.5 t.
**61873 – 61880. MBSO.** Dia. ED203. Lot No. 30642 Wolverton 1961. 72S. 54.5 t.
**75661 – 75678. DTBSO.** Dia. EG203. Lot No. 30608 Wolverton 1960 – 61. 82S. 32.5 t.
**75858 – 75865. DTBSO.** Dia. EG203. Lot No. 30643 Wolverton 1961. 82S. 32.5 t.

| 304 017 | | RCLG | LG | 75681 61629 75661 |
|---------|------|------|----|-----|
| 304 019 | **RR** | RCLG | LG | 75683 61631 75663 |
| 304 021 | | RCLG | LG | 75685 61633 75665 |
| 304 024 | | RCLG | LG | 75688 61636 75668 |
| 304 027 | | RCLG | LG | 75691 61639 75671 |
| 304 029 | | RCLG | LG | 75693 61641 75673 |
| 304 030 | | RCLG | LG | 75694 61642 75674 |
| 304 032 | | RCLG | LG | 75696 61644 75676 |
| 304 033 | | RCLG | LG | 75697 61645 75677 |

| 304 034 | RR | RCLG | LG | 75698 61646 75678 |
| 304 036 | RR | RCLG | LG | 75868 61873 75858 |
| 304 037 | RR | RCLG | LG | 75869 61874 75859 |
| 304 040 | RR | RCLG | LG | 75872 61877 75862 |
| 304 042 | | RCLG | LG | 75874 61879 75864 |
| 304 043 | | RCLG | LG | 75875 61880 75865 |

# CLASS 305/1

BDTSO – MBSO – DTSO. All facelifted with fluorescent lighting and PA.
**Bogies:** Gresley.
**Gangways:** None.
**Traction Motors:** Four GEC WT380 of 153 kW.
**Dimensions:** 19.53 x 2.82 m (outer cars), 19.34 x 2.82 m (inner cars).
**Maximum Speed:** 75 mph.

**BDTSO.** Dia. EF205. Lot No. 30570 York 1960. 34.9 t. 92S.
**MBSO.** Dia. ED204. Lot No. 30571 York 1960. 56.4 t. 84S.
**DTSO.** Dia. EE209. Lot No. 30572 York 1960. 31.5 t. 92S.

| 305 401 | | N | NNEX | IL | 75462 61429 75514 |
| 305 403 | (305 445) | | NNEX | EM | 75506 61473 75558 |
| 305 404 | (305 447) | | RFXX | GW | 75508 61475 75560 |
| 305 410 | | N | NNEX | EM | 75471 61438 75523 |
| 305 412 | | | NNEX | EM | 75473 61440 75525 |
| 305 416 | | | NNEX | EM | 75477 61444 75529 |
| 305 417 | | | NNEX | EM | 75478 61445 75530 |
| 305 420 | | | NNEX | EM | 75481 61448 75533 |
| Spare | | | RAGW | GW | 61476 |

# CLASS 305/2

BDTCOL – MBSO – TSOL – DTSO. All facelifted with fluorescent lighting, new seats and PA.
**Bogies:** Gresley.
**Gangways:** Originally non-gangwayed, but now gangwayed within unit.
**Traction Motors:** Four GEC WT380 of 153 kW.
**Dimensions:** 19.53 x 2.82 m (outer cars), 19.36 x 2.82 m (inner cars).
**Maximum Speed:** 75 mph.

**BDTCOL.** Dia. EF304. Lot No. 30566 York/Doncaster 1960. 24F 52S 1L. 36.5 t.
**MBSO.** Dia. ED216. Lot No. 30567 York/Doncaster 1960. 76S. 56.5 t.
**TSOL.** Dia. EH223. Lot No. 30568 York/Doncaster 1960. 86S 1L. 31.5 t.
**DTSO.** Dia. EE220. Lot No. 30569 York/Doncaster 1960. 88S. 32.7 t.

| 305 501 | RS | RAGW | GW | 75424 61410 70356 75443 |
| 305 502 | RS | RAGW | GW | 75425 61421 70357 75444 |
| 305 503 | RS | RCLG | LG | 75426 61412 | 75445 |
| 305 504 | RS | RCLG | LG | 75427 61413 | 75446 |
| 305 506 | RS | RCLG | LG | 75429 61415 | 75448 |
| 305 507 | RS | RCLG | LG | 75430 61416 | 75449 |
| 305 508 | RS | RAGW | GW | 75431 61417 70363 75450 |
| 305 509 | RS | RCLG | LG | 75432 61418 | 75451 |
| 305 510 | RS | RCLG | LG | 75433 61419 | 75452 |

| 305 511 | **RS** RCLG | LG | 75434 | 61420 | | 75453 |
|---------|-------------|-----|-------|-------|-------|-------|
| 305 513 | **RS** RCLG | LG | 75436 | 61422 | | 75455 |
| 305 514 | **N** RCLG | LG | 75437 | 61423 | | 75456 |
| 305 515 | **RS** RCLG | LG | 75438 | 61424 | | 75457 |
| 305 516 | **RS** RCLG | LG | 75439 | 61425 | | 75458 |
| 305 517 | **RS** RAGW | GW | 75440 | 61426 | 70372 | 75459 |
| 305 518 | **RS** RCLG | LG | 75441 | 61427 | | 75460 |
| 305 519 | **RS** RAGW | GW | 75442 | 61428 | 70374 | 75461 |

**Spare TSOL (DTSO\*)**

| 70359 | 70361 | 70364 | 70366 | 70370 | 70371 | 70373 | 70360 |
|-------|-------|-------|-------|-------|-------|-------|-------|
| 70360 | 70362 | 70365 | 70369 | | | | |

# CLASS 305/3

BDTSO – MBSO – TCsoL – DTSO. New batch formed by strengthening class 305/1 with Class 302 TCsoL (which have since been removed). All facelifted with fluorescent lighting, new seats and PA.
**Bogies:** Gresley.
**Gangways:** None.
**Traction Motors:** Four GEC WT380 of 153 kW.
**Dimensions:** 19.53 x 2.82 m (outer cars), 19.36 x 2.82 m (inner cars).
**Maximum Speed:** 75 mph.

**BDTSO.** Dia. EF205. Lot No. 30570 York 1960. 34.9 t. 92S.
**MBSO.** Dia. ED204. Lot No. 30571 York 1960. 56.4 t. 84S.
**DTSO.** Dia. EE209. Lot No. 30572 York 1960. 31.5 t. 92S.

| 305 521 | (305 403) | **N** | RFXX | | 75464 | 61431 | 75516 |
|---------|-----------|-------|------|-----|-------|-------|-------|
| 305 525 | (305 419) | **N** | NNEX | EM | 75480 | 61447 | 75532 |
| 305 526 | (305 422) | **N** | RFXX | | 75483 | 61450 | 75535 |
| 305 527 | (305 446) | **N** | NNEX | EM | 75507 | 61474 | 75559 |
| 305 528 | (305 451) | **N** | NNEX | EM | 75512 | 61479 | 75564 |

# CLASS 305/2

BDTCOL – MBSO – TSOL – DTSO. These sets are Class 302 units with power cars from Class 305/1. All facelifted with fluorescent lighting, new seats and PA.
**Gangways:** None.
**Traction Motors:** Four GEC WT380 of 153 kW.
**Dimensions:** 19.36 x 2.82 m.
**Maximum Speed:** 75 mph.

**75090 – 75199. BDTCOL.** Lot No. 30436. York/Doncaster 1958 – 59. Dia. EF303. 24F 52S 1L. 39.5 t. B5 bogies.
**75356. BDTCOL.** Lot No. 30440. York/Doncaster 1959. Dia. EF303. 24F 52S 1L. 39.5 t. B5 bogies.
**MBSO.** Dia. ED204. Lot No. 30571 York 1960. 56.4 t. 84S.
**70065 – 70088. TSOL.** Lot No. 30437. York/Doncaster 1958 – 59. Dia. EH223. 86S 1L. 34.4 t. B4 bogies.
**70224. TSOL.** Lot No. 30441. York 1959 – 61. Dia. EH223. 86S 1L. 34.4 t. B4 bogies.

**75038 – 75073. DTSO.** Lot No. 30435. York 1958 – 59. Dia. EE219. 88S. 33.4 t. B4 or B5 bogies.
**75281. DTSO.** Lot No. 30439. York 1959 – 60. Dia. EE219. 88S. 33.4 t. B4 or B5 bogies.

| | | | | | | | | |
|---|---|---|---|---|---|---|---|---|
| 305 594 | (302 226) | **N** | NNEX | EM | 75199 | 61430 | 70088 | 75073 |
| 305 595 | (302 220) | **N** | NNEX | EM | 75193 | 61446 | 70079 | 75067 |
| 305 596 | (302 208) | **N** | NNEX | EM | 75356 | 61480 | 70224 | 75281 |
| 305 597 | (302 222) | **N** | NNEX | EM | 75195 | 61433 | 70081 | 75069 |
| 305 598 | (302 217) | **N** | NNEX | EM | 75190 | 61435 | 70076 | 75064 |
| 305 599 | (302 206) | **N** | NNEX | EM | 75090 | 61434 | 70065 | 75038 |

# CLASS 306

. DMSO – TBSO – DTSO. Converted 1960 – 1 from 1500 V d.c. Kept for special workings. LNER design. Sliding doors. Screw couplings.
**Bogies:** LNER bogies.
**Gangways:** None.
**Traction Motors:** Four Crompton Parkinson of 155 kW.
**Dimensions:** 18.41 x 2.90 m (DMSO), 16.78 x 2.90 m (TBSO), 16.87 x 2.90 m (DTSO).
**Maximum Speed:** 65 mph.
**Non-standard Livery:** Original BR multiple unit green.

**DMSO.** Dia. EA217. Lot No. 363 Metro-Cammell. 1949. 51.7 t. 62S.
**TBSO.** Dia. EJ201. Lot No. 364 1949. Metro-Cammell. 26.4 t. 46S.
**DTSO.** Dia. EE211. Lot No. 365 1949. BRCW. 27.9 t. 60S.

| | | | | | | |
|---|---|---|---|---|---|---|
| 306 017 | **0** | NGEX | IL | 65217 | 65417 | 65617 |

# CLASS 307

BDTBSO – MSO – TSO – DTCOL. 25 kV a.c. overhead. Converted 1960 – 1 from 1500 V d.c. All refurbished with new seats, fluorescent lighting, PA.
**Bogies:** Gresley (MSO), B4 (TSO and DTCO) B5 (BDTBSO).
**Gangways:** Originally non-gangwayed, but now gangwayed within unit.
**Traction Motors:** Four GEC WT344 of 130 kW.
**Dimensions:** 19.50 x 2.83 m.
**Maximum Speed:** 75 mph.

**BDTBSO.** Dia. EO202. Lot No. 30205 Ashford/Eastleigh 1954 – 6. 66S. 43 t.
**MSO.** Dia. EC204. Lot No. 30203 Ashford/Eastleigh 1954 – 6. 86S. 47.5 t.
**TSOL.** Dia. EH222. Lot No. 30204 Ashford/Eastleigh 1954 – 6. 86S 1L. 31 t.
**DTCOL.** Dia. EE307. Lot No. 30206 Afd./Elh 1954 – 6. 24F 52S 1L. 33 t.

M Stored at MoD Kineton (near Fenny Compton).

| | | | | | | | |
|---|---|---|---|---|---|---|---|
| 307 102 | **N** | PPMB | M (S) | 75002 | 61002 | 70002 | 75102 |
| 307 103 | | PPMB | M (S) | 75003 | 61003 | 70003 | 75103 |
| 307 104 | | PPMB | M (S) | 75004 | 61004 | 70004 | 75104 |
| 307 105 | **Y** | PPMB | M (S) | 75030 | 61005 | 70005 | 75122 |
| 307 107 | | PPMB | M (S) | 75007 | 61007 | 70007 | 75107 |
| 307 108 | | PPMB | M (S) | 75008 | 61008 | 70008 | 75108 |
| 307 109 | | PPMB | M (S) | 75009 | 61009 | 70009 | 75109 |

| 307 110 | | PPMB | M (S) | 75010 61010 70010 75110 |
| 307 111 | Y | PPMB | M (S) | 75011 61011 70011 75111 |
| 307 112 | | PPMB | M (S) | 75012 61012 70012 75112 |
| 307 113 | | PPMB | M (S) | 75013 61013 70013 75113 |
| 307 114 | | PPMB | M (S) | 75014 61014 70014 75114 |
| 307 115 | | PPMB | M (S) | 75015 61015 70015 75115 |
| 307 116 | | PPMB | M (S) | 75016 61016 70018 75116 |
| 307 117 | N | PPMB | M (S) | 75017 61017 70017 75117 |
| 307 119 | | PPMB | M (S) | 75019 61019 70019 75119 |
| 307 120 | Y | PPMB | M (S) | 75020 61030 70020 75130 |
| 307 122 | Y | PPMB | M (S) | 75022 61022 70022 75120 |
| 307 123 | | PPMB | M (S) | 75023 61023 70023 75123 |
| 307 124 | N | PPMB | M (S) | 75024 61024 70024 75124 |
| 307 125 | | PPMB | M (S) | 75025 61025 70025 75125 |
| 307 126 | N | PPMB | M (S) | 75026 61026 70026 75126 |
| 307 127 | | PPMB | M (S) | 75027 61027 70027 75127 |
| 307 128 | | PPMB | M (S) | 75028 61028 70028 75128 |
| 307 129 | | PPMB | M (S) | 75029 61029 70029 75129 |
| 307 130 | Y | PPMB | M (S) | 75005 61020 70030 75105 |
| 307 131 | | PPMB | M (S) | 75031 61031 70031 75131 |
| 307 132 | N | PPMB | M (S) | 75032 61032 70032 75132 |

# CLASS 308

BDTCOL – MBSO – TSOL – DTSO. Refurbished with new seats, fluorescent lighting and pa.
**Bogies:** Gresley.
**Gangways:** Originally non-gangwayed, but now gangwayed within unit.
**Traction Motors:** Four English Electric 536A of 143.5 kW.
**Dimensions:** 19.36 x 2.82 m (outer cars), 19.35 x 2.82 m (inner cars).
**Maximum Speed:** 75 mph.

**75878 – 75886. BDTCOL.** Dia. EF304. Lot No. 30652 Yk 1961. 24F 52S 1L. 36.3 t.
**75896 – 75919. BDTCOL.** Dia. EF304. Lot No. 30656 Yk 1961. 24F 52S 1L. 36.3 t.
**75435. BDTCOL.** Dia. EF304. Lot No. 30566 York/Doncaster 1960. 24F 52S 1L. 36.5 t.
**61883 – 61891. MBSO.** Dia. ED216. Lot No. 30653 York 1961. 76S. 55.0 t.
**61892 – 61915. MBSO.** Dia. ED216. Lot No. 30657 York 1961. 76S. 55.0 t.
**70367. TSOL.** Dia. EH223. Lot No. 30568 York/Doncaster 1960. 86S 1L. 31.4 t.
**70611 – 70619. TSOL.** Dia. EH223. Lot No. 30654 York 1961. 86S 1L. 31.4 t.
**70620 – 70643. TSOL.** Dia. EH223. Lot No. 30658 York 1961. 86S 1L. 31.4 t.
**75887 – 75895. DTSO.** Dia. EE220. Lot No. 30655 York 1961. 88S. 33 t.
**75929 – 75952. DTSO.** Dia. EE220. Lot No. 30659 York 1961. 88S. 33 t.

* Class 305/1 car.

| 308 133 | N | NTSX | EM | 75878 61883 70611 75887 |
| 308 134 | N | NTSX | EM | 75879 61884 70612 75888 |
| 308 136 | N | NTSX | EM | 75881 61886 70614 75890 |
| 308 137 | N | NTSX | EM | 75882 61887 70615 75891 |

| 308 138 |   | N | NTSX | EM     | 75883 61888 70367 75892 |
|---------|---|---|------|--------|-------------------------|
| 308 139 |   | N | NTSX | EM     | 75884 61889 70617 75893 |
| 308 140 |   | N | NTSX | EM     | 75885 61890 70618 75894 |
| 308 141 |   | N | NTSX | EM     | 75886 61891 70619 75895 |
| 308 142 |   | N | NTSX | EM     | 75896 61892 70620 75929 |
| 308 143 |   | N | NTSX | EM     | 75897 61893 70621 75930 |
| 308 144 | * | N | NTSX | EM     | 75435 61894 70622 75931 |
| 308 145 |   | N | NTSX | EM     | 75899 61895 70623 75932 |
| 308 146 |   | N | NTSX | EM     | 75900 61896 70624 75933 |
| 308 147 |   | N | NTSX | EM     | 75901 61897 70625 75934 |
| 308 148 |   | N | NTSX | EM     | 75902 61898 70626 75935 |
| 308 149 |   | N | NTSX | EM     | 75903 61899 70627 75936 |
| 308 150 |   | N | NTSX | EM     | 75904 61900 70628 75937 |
| 308 151 |   | N | NTSX | EM     | 75905 61901 70629 75938 |
| 308 152 |   | N | NTSX | EM     | 75906 61902 70630 75939 |
| 308 153 |   | N | NTSX | EM     | 75907 61903 70631 75940 |
| 308 154 |   | N | NTSX | EM     | 75908 61904 70632 75941 |
| 308 155 |   | N | NTSX | EM     | 75909 61905 70633 75942 |
| 308 156 |   | N | NTSX | EM     | 75880 61906 70613 75889 |
| 308 157 |   | N | NTSX | EM     | 75911 61907 70635 75944 |
| 308 158 |   | N | NTSX | EM     | 75912 61908 70636 75945 |
| 308 159 |   | N | NTSX | EM     | 75913 61909 70637 75946 |
| 308 160 |   | N | NTSX | EM     | 75914 61910 70638 75947 |
| 308 161 |   | N | NTSX | EM     | 75915 61911 70639 75948 |
| 308 162 |   | N | NTSX | EM     | 75916 61912 70640 75949 |
| 308 163 |   | N | NTSX | EM     | 75917 61913 70641 75950 |
| 308 164 |   | N | NTSX | EM     | 75918 61914 70642 75951 |
| 308 165 |   | N | NTSX | EM     | 75919 61915 70643 75952 |
| Spare   |   |   | NTSX | EM (U) | 75898                   |

# CLASS 309/1        ESSEX EXPRESS STOCK

DMBSO(T) – TSOL – TCsoL – BDTSOL. Built 1962 – 3 as 2 car units. Made up to four cars by the conversion of loco-hauled stock in 1973/80 – 1. All now refurbished with fluorescent lighting, hopper ventilators, new seating, PA.
**Bogies:** Commonwealth.
**Gangways:** Throughout.
**Traction Motors:** Four GEC of 210 kW.
**Dimensions:** 19.76 x 2.82 m (outer cars), 19.67 x 2.82 m (inner cars).
**Maximum Speed:** 100 mph.

**DMBSO(T).** Dia. EB206. Lot No. 30684 York 1962 – 63. 44S. 60 t.
**71107 – 71110. TSOL.** Dia. EH227. Lot No. 30871 W'ton 1973 – 74. 64S 2L. 35 t.
**71569 – 71572. TSOL.** Dia. EH227. Lot No. 30954 W'ton 1978 – 81. 64S 2L. 35 t.
**71111 – 71114. TCsoL.** Dia. EH309. Lot No. 30872 Wolverton 1973 – 74. 24F 28S 1L. 36 t.
**71573 – 71576. TCsoL.** Dia. EH309. Lot No. 30954 Wolverton 1978 – 81. 24F 28S 1L. 36 t.
**BDTSOL.** Dia. EF213. Lot No. 30683 York 1960 – 62. 60S 1L. 40 t.

Note: 61940/2 are DMBSO and seat 52S.

| 309 601 | N | NGEX | CC | 61940 71569 71573 75984 |
|---|---|---|---|---|
| 309 602 | N | NGEX | CC | 61941 71570 71574 75985 |
| 309 603 | N | NGEX | CC | 61942 71571 71575 75986 |
| 309 604 | N | NGEX | CC | 61943 71572 71576 75987 |
| 309 605 | N | NGEX | CC | 61944 71108 71113 75988 |
| 309 606 | N | NGEX | CC | 61945 71109 71112 75989 |
| 309 607 | N | NGEX | CC | 61946 71107 71111 75990 |
| 309 608 | N | NGEX | CC | 61947 71110 71114 75991 |

# CLASS 309/2      ESSEX EXPRESS STOCK

BDTCsoL – MBSOL(T) – TSO – DTSOL. Built 1962 – 3 as 2 car units. Units 309 611 – 309 618 formerly contained griddle cars, but these were withdrawn and their place has been taken by the conversion of loco-hauled TSOs on refurbishment. All refurbished with fluorescent lighting, hopper ventilators, new seating, PA.
**Bogies:** Commonwealth.
**Gangways:** Throughout.
**Traction Motors:** Four GEC of 210 kW.
**Dimensions:** 19.76 x 2.82 m (outer cars), 19.67 x 2.82 m (inner cars).
**Maximum Speed:** 100 mph.

**75638 – 44. BDTCsoL.** Dia. EF301. Lot No. 30679 York 1962. 18F 32S 2L. 40 t.
**75963 – 67. BDTCsoL.** Dia. EF213. Lot No. 30675 York 1962. 18F 32S 2L. 40 t.
**61926 – 31. MBSO(T).** Dia. ED209. Lot No. 30676 York 1962. 44S 2L. 58 t.
**61933 – 39. MBSO(T).** Dia. ED209. Lot No. 30680 York 1962. 44S 2L. 58 t.
**70254 – 59. TSO.** Dia. EH229. Lot No. 30677 York 1962. 68S 35 t.
**71755 – 61. TSO.** Dia. EH228. Lot No. 31001 Wolverton 1984 – 87. 68S. 35 t.
**75970 – 75. DTSOL.** Dia. EF213. Lot No. 30678 York 1962. 56S 2L 37 t.
**75977 – 83. DTSOL.** Dia. EF213. Lot No. 30682 York 1962 – 1963. 56S 2L. 37 t.

61933/29/30/31 are MBSO and seat 48S 2L.

| 309 612 | N | NGEX | CC | 75638 61933 71755 75977 |
|---|---|---|---|---|
| 309 613 | N | NGEX | CC | 75639 61934 71756 75978 |
| 309 616 | N | NGEX | CC | 75642 61937 71759 75981 |
| 309 617 | N | NGEX | CC | 75643 61938 71760 75982 |
| 309 618 | N | NGEX | CC | 75966 61939 71761 75983 |
| 309 624 | N | NGEX | CC | 75965 61928 70256 75972 |
| 309 625 | N | NGEX | CC | 75641 61927 71758 75973 |
| 309 626 | N | NGEX | CC | 75967 61930 70258 75974 |
| 309 627 | N | NGEX | CC | 75644 61931 70259 75975 |

Former numbers of converted hauled stock:

| 71107 (26203) | 71113 (16244) | 71573 (16264) | 71756 ( 5068) |
|---|---|---|---|
| 71108 (26189) | 71114 (16252) | 71574 (16257) | 71758 ( 5058) |
| 71109 (26196) | 71569 ( 5047) | 71575 (16242) | 71759 ( 5062) |
| 71110 (26204) | 71570 ( 5050) | 71576 (16259) | 71760 ( 5056) |
| 71111 (16246) | 71571 ( 5059) | 71755 ( 5051) | 71761 ( 5066) |
| 71112 (16249) | 71572 ( 5061) | | |

# CLASS 310

Disc brakes. All facelifted. with new panels and PA.
**Bogies:** B4.
**Gangways:** Within unit.
**Traction Motors:** Four EE546 of 201.5 kW.
**Dimensions:** 19.86 x 2.82 m (outer cars), 19.93 x 2.82 m (inner cars).
**Maximum Speed:** 75 mph.

**BDTSOL.** Dia. EF211. Lot No. 30745 Derby 1965 – 67. 80S 2L. 37.3 t.
**76228. BDTSOL.** Formerly a DTCOL to Lot 39748. Dia. EF210. Seats 68S 2L.
**76998. BDTSOL.** Rebuilt from TSO 70756 to Lot 30747. Dia. EF214. Seats 75S 2L.
**MBSO.** Dia. ED219. Lot No. 30746 Derby 1965 – 67. 68S. 57.2 t.
**TSO.** Dia. EH232. Lot No. 30747 Derby 1965 – 67. 98S. 31.7 t.
**DTCOL (310/0).** Dia. EE306. Lot No. 30748 Derby 1965 – 67. 25F 43S 2L. 34.4 t.
**DTSOL (310/1).** Dia. EE237. Lot No. 30748 Derby 1965 – 67. 75S 2L. 34.4 t.

**Class 310/0.** BDTSOL – MBSO – TSO – DTCOL.

| | | | | | | |
|---|---|---|---|---|---|---|
| 310 046 | N | NTSX | EM | 76130 | 62071 | 70731 76180 |
| 310 047 | N | NTSX | EM | 76131 | 62072 | 70732 76181 |
| 310 049 | N | NTSX | EM | 76133 | 62074 | 70734 76183 |
| 310 050 | N | NTSX | EM | 76134 | 62075 | 70735 76184 |
| 310 051 | N | NTSX | EM | 76135 | 62076 | 70736 76185 |
| 310 052 | N | NTSX | EM | 76136 | 62077 | 70737 76186 |
| 310 056 | N | NTSX | EM | 76140 | 62081 | 70741 76190 |
| 310 057 | N | NTSX | EM | 76141 | 62082 | 70742 76191 |
| 310 058 | N | NTSX | EM | 76142 | 62083 | 70743 76192 |
| 310 059 | N | NTSX | EM | 76143 | 62084 | 70744 76205 |
| 310 061 | N | NTSX | EM | 76144 | 62085 | 70745 76194 |
| 310 064 | N | NTSX | EM | 76145 | 62086 | 70746 76195 |
| 310 065 | N | NTSX | EM | 76148 | 62089 | 70749 76198 |
| 310 066 | N | NTSX | EM | 76149 | 62090 | 70750 76199 |
| 310 067 | N | NTSX | EM | 76228 | 62091 | 70751 76200 |
| 310 068 | N | NTSX | EM | 76151 | 62092 | 70752 76201 |
| 310 069 | N | NTSX | EM | 76152 | 62093 | 70753 76202 |
| 310 070 | N | NTSX | EM | 76153 | 62094 | 70754 76203 |
| 310 074 | N | NTSX | EM | 76154 | 62095 | 70755 76204 |
| 310 075 | N | NTSX | EM | 76158 | 62099 | 70759 76208 |
| 310 077 | N | NTSX | EM | 76159 | 62100 | 70760 76209 |
| 310 079 | N | NTSX | EM | 76161 | 62102 | 70762 76211 |
| 310 080 | N | NTSX | EM | 76163 | 62104 | 70764 76213 |
| 310 081 | N | NTSX | EM | 76164 | 62105 | 70765 76214 |
| 310 082 | N | NTSX | EM | 76165 | 62106 | 70766 76215 |
| 310 083 | N | NTSX | EM | 76166 | 62107 | 70767 76216 |
| 310 084 | N | NTSX | EM | 76167 | 62108 | 70768 76217 |
| 310 085 | N | NTSX | EM | 76168 | 62109 | 70769 76218 |
| 310 086 | N | NTSX | EM | 76169 | 62110 | 70770 76219 |
| 310 087 | N | NTSX | EM | 76170 | 62111 | 70771 76220 |
| | | | | 76171 | 62112 | 70772 76221 |

| 310 088 | N | NTSX | EM | 76172 62113 70773 76222 |
|---|---|---|---|---|
| 310 089 | N | NTSX | EM | 76173 62114 70774 76223 |
| 310 091 | N | NTSX | EM | 76175 62116 70776 76225 |
| 310 092 | N | NTSX | EM | 76176 62117 70777 76226 |
| 310 093 | N | NTSX | EM | 76177 62118 70778 76227 |
| 310 094 | N | NTSX | EM | 76998 62119 70780 76193 |
| 310 095 | N | RDBY | BY | 76179 62120 70779 76229 |

**Class 310/1.** BDTSOL – MBSO – TSO – DTSOL. ·

| 310 101 | (310 073) | PM | RDBY | BY | 76157 62098 70758 76207 |
|---|---|---|---|---|---|
| 310 102 | (310 055) | PM | RDBY | BY | 76139 62080 70740 76189 |
| 310 103 | (310 076) | PM | RDBY | BY | 76160 62101 70761 76210 |
| 310 104 | (310 078) | PM | RDBY | BY | 76162 62103 70763 76212 |
| 310 105 | (310 090) | PM | RDBY | BY | 76174 62115 70775 76224 |
| 310 106 | (310 072) | PM | RDBY | BY | 76156 62097 70757 76206 |
| 310 107 | (310 062) | PM | RDBY | BY | 76146 62087 70747 76196 |
| 310 108 | (310 048) | PM | RDBY | BY | 76132 62073 70733 76182 |
| 310 109 | (310 053) | PM | RDBY | BY | 76137 62078 70738 76187 |
| 310 110 | (310 054) | PM | RDBY | BY | 76138 62079 70739 76188 |
| 310 111 | (310 063) | PM | RDBY | BY | 76147 62088 70748 76197 |

# CLASS 311

DTSO – MBSO – BDTSO. Sliding doors.
**Bogies:** Gresley.
**Gangways:** Non-gangwayed.
**Traction Motors:** Four AEI 165 kW.
**Dimensions:** 19.50 x 2.82 m (outer cars), 19.36 x 2.82 m (inner cars).
**Maximum Speed:** 75 mph.

**DTSO.** Dia. EE214. Lot No. 30767 Cravens 1967. 83S. 34.4 t.
**MBSO.** Dia. ED211. Lot No. 30768 Cravens 1967. 70S. 56.4 t.
**BDTSO.** Dia. EF212. Lot No. 30769 Cravens 1967. 83S. 38.4 t.

| 311 103 | RAGW | GW | 76414 62174 76433 |
|---|---|---|---|
| 311 104 | RAGW | GW | 76415 62175 76434 |

# CLASS 312

BDTSOL – MBSO – TSO – DTCOL. Disc brakes PA.
**Bogies:** B4.
**Gangways:** Within unit.
**Traction Motors:** Four EE546 of 201.5 kW.
**Dimensions:** 19.86 x 2.82 m (outer cars), 19.93 x 2.82 m (inner cars).
**Maximum Speed:** 90 mph.

**Class 312/0.** Standard design.

**76994 – 97 BDTSOL.** Dia. EF213. Lot No. 30891 York 1976. 84S 1L. 34.9 t.
**62657 – 60 MBSO.** Dia. ED214. Lot No. 30892 York 1976. 68S. 56 t.
**71277 – 80 TSO.** Dia. EH209. Lot No. 30893 York 1976. 98S. 30.5 t.
**78045 – 48 DTCOL.** Dia. EE305. Lot No. 30894 York 1976. 25F 47S 2L.
**76949 – 74 BDTSOL.** Dia. EF213. Lot No. 30863 York 1977 – 78. 84S 1L. 34.9 t.
**62484 – 509 MBSO.** Dia. ED212. Lot No. 30864 York 1977 – 78. 68S. 56 t.

Network-SouthEast liveried Class 302 No. 302 203 passes Limehouse on 19th September 1992.                                                                    *Norman Barrington*

Class 303 No. 303 014 in Strathclyde PTE livery at Partick on 25th May 1991.
*Norman Barrington*

▲ Class 304 No. 304 045 near Cliff Vale (Stoke) whilst working the 11.33 Manchester Piccadilly – Stoke-on-Trent service on 6th December 1991.
*Hugh Ballantyne*

▼ Regional Railways liveried Class 305 No. 305 514 departing from Crewe on 29th August 1992 with a Manchester service.
*John Augustson*

▲ Class 308 No. 308 150 pauses at Barking on 19th September 1991 whilst forming a Shoeburyness service. *Norman Barrington*

▼ Class 309 Clacton Express unit No. 309 618 forms the 09.04 Liverpool Street – Clacton at Marks Tay on 14th May 1992. *Brian Denton*

▲ Class 310 No. 310 087 at Barking with a London service on 17th July 1990.
*Norman Barrington*

▼ Class 312 No. 312 792 at Barking with a London service on 31st March 1992.
*Norman Barrington*

▲ Dual voltage Class 313 No. 313 003 at Gospel Oak on 29th August 1992 whilst forming the 13.03 Richmond – North Woolwich.    *Kevin Conkey*

▼ Class 314 No. 314 206 pauses at Dalmuir with the 15.54 Helensburgh – Airdrie on 21st May 1990.    *Tom Heavyside*

▲ Class 317 No. 317 319 passing Great Chesterford as the 15.02 Liverpoo Street – Cambridge on 25th March 1991.  *Hugh Ballantyne*

▼ Class 318 No. 318 250 leaves Irvine with the 17.30 Glasgow Central – Ay on 2nd August 1990.  *John Augustson*

▲ Class 319/1 No. 319 174 at Cricklewood on 1st September 1992 whilst forming the 12.48 Bedford – Brighton.                                    *Kevin Conkey*

▼ Class 321 No. 321 356 passing through Stratford on 17th October 1992 with a Liverpool Street service.                                         *Kevin Conkey*

▲ Also at Stratford Class 322 No. 322 482 forms the 10.30 Stansted Airport – Liverpool Street service on 21st May 1992. *Brian Denton*

▼ Class 323 No. 323 201 in Centro livery stands outside the works of Hunslet TPL. These units will enter service shortly on the Cross City line between Lichfield and Redditch. *Hunslet TPL*

**71168 – 93 TSO.** Dia. EH209. Lot No. 30865 York 1977 – 78. 98S. 30.5 t.
**78000 – 25 DTCOL.** Dia. EE305. Lot No. 30866 York 1977 – 78. 25F 47S 2L.

**Notes:** 312 727 – 730 were formerly numbered 312 201 – 204.

| | | | | | | |
|---|---|---|---|---|---|---|
| 312 701 | **N** | NGEX | CC | 76949 | 62484 | 71168 78000 |
| 312 702 | **N** | NGEX | CC | 76950 | 62485 | 71169 78001 |
| 312 703 | **N** | NGEX | CC | 76951 | 62486 | 71170 78002 |
| 312 704 | **N** | NGEX | CC | 76952 | 62487 | 71171 78003 |
| 312 705 | **N** | NGEX | CC | 76953 | 62488 | 71172 78004 |
| 312 706 | **N** | NGEX | CC | 76954 | 62489 | 71173 78005 |
| 312 707 | **N** | NGEX | CC | 76955 | 62490 | 71174 78006 |
| 312 708 | **N** | NGEX | CC | 76956 | 62491 | 71175 78007 |
| 312 709 | **N** | NGEX | CC | 76957 | 62492 | 71176 78008 |
| 312 710 | **N** | NGEX | CC | 76958 | 62493 | 71177 78009 |
| 312 711 | **N** | NGEX | CC | 76959 | 62494 | 71178 78010 |
| 312 712 | **N** | NGEX | CC | 76960 | 62495 | 71179 78011 |
| 312 713 | **N** | NGEX | CC | 76961 | 62496 | 71180 78012 |
| 312 714 | **N** | NGEX | CC | 76962 | 62497 | 71181 78013 |
| 312 715 | **N** | NGEX | CC | 76963 | 62498 | 71182 78014 |
| 312 716 | **N** | NGEX | CC | 76964 | 62499 | 71183 78015 |
| 312 717 | **N** | NGEX | CC | 76965 | 62500 | 71184 78016 |
| 312 718 | **N** | NGEX | CC | 76966 | 62501 | 71185 78017 |
| 312 719 | **N** | NGEX | CC | 76967 | 62502 | 71186 78018 |
| 312 720 | **N** | NGEX | CC | 76968 | 62503 | 71187 78019 |
| 312 721 | **N** | NGEX | CC | 76969 | 62504 | 71188 78020 |
| 312 722 | **N** | NGEX | CC | 76970 | 62505 | 71189 78021 |
| 312 723 | **N** | NGEX | CC | 76971 | 62506 | 71190 78022 |
| 312 724 | **N** | NGEX | CC | 76972 | 62507 | 71191 78023 |
| 312 725 | **N** | NGEX | CC | 76973 | 62508 | 71192 78024 |
| 312 726 | **N** | NGEX | CC | 76974 | 62509 | 71193 78025 |
| 312 727 | **N** | NGEX | CC | 76994 | 62657 | 71277 78045 |
| 312 728 | **N** | NGEX | CC | 76995 | 62658 | 71278 78046 |
| 312 729 | **N** | NGEX | CC | 76996 | 62659 | 71279 78047 |
| 312 730 | **N** | NGEX | CC | 76997 | 62660 | 71280 78048 |

**Class 312/1.** Can also operate on 6.25 kV a.c. overhead.

**BDTSOL.** Dia. EF213. Lot No. 30867 York 1975 – 76. 84S 2L. 34.9 t.
**MBSO.** Dia. ED213. Lot No. 30868 York 1975 – 76. 68S. 56 t.
**TSO.** Dia. EH209. Lot No. 30869 York 1975 – 76. 98S. 30.5 t.
**DTCOL.** Dia. EE305. Lot No. 30870 York 1975 – 76. 25F 47S 2L.

| | | | | | | |
|---|---|---|---|---|---|---|
| 312 781 | **N** | NGEX | CC | 76975 | 62510 | 71194 78026 |
| 312 782 | **N** | NGEX | CC | 76976 | 62511 | 71195 78027 |
| 312 783 | **N** | NGEX | CC | 76977 | 62512 | 71196 78028 |
| 312 784 | **N** | NGEX | CC | 76978 | 62513 | 71197 78029 |
| 312 785 | **N** | NGEX | CC | 76979 | 62514 | 71198 78030 |
| 312 786 | **N** | NTSX | EM | 76980 | 62515 | 71199 78031 |
| 312 787 | **N** | NTSX | EM | 76981 | 62516 | 71200 78032 |
| 312 788 | **N** | NTSX | EM | 76982 | 62517 | 71201 78033 |
| 312 789 | **N** | NTSX | EM | 76983 | 62518 | 71202 78034 |
| 312 790 | **N** | NTSX | EM | 76984 | 62519 | 71203 78035 |
| 312 791 | **N** | NTSX | EM | 76985 | 62520 | 71204 78036 |

| 312 792 | N | NTSX | EM | 76986 62521 71205 78037 |
|---|---|---|---|---|
| 312 793 | N | NTSX | EM | 76987 62522 71206 78038 |
| 312 794 | N | NTSX | EM | 76988 62523 71207 78039 |
| 312 795 | N | NTSX | EM | 76989 62524 71208 78040 |
| 312 796 | N | NTSX | EM | 76990 62525 71209 78041 |
| 312 797 | N | NTSX | EM | 76991 62526 71210 78042 |
| 312 798 | N | NTSX | EM | 76992 62527 71211 78043 |
| 312 799 | N | NTSX | EM | 76993 62528 71212 78044 |

# CLASS 313

DMSO – PTSO – BDMSO. Tightlock couplers. Sliding doors. Disc and rheostatic brakes. PA. Cab to shore radio.
**System:** 25 kV a.c. overhead/750 V d.c. third rail.
**Bogies:** BX1.
**Gangways:** Within unit. End doors.
**Traction Motors:** Four GEC G310AZ of 82.125 kW.
**Dimensions:** 19.80 x 2.82 m (outer cars), 19.92 x 2.82 m (inner cars).
**Maximum Speed:** 75 mph.

**DMSO (A).** Dia. EA204. Lot No. 30879 York 1976 – 77. 74S. 36.4 t.
**PTSO.** Dia. EH210. Lot No. 30880 York 1976 – 77. 84S. 30.5 t.
**DMSO (B).** Dia. EI201. Lot No. 30885 York 1976 – 77. 74S. 37.6 t.

* – Extra shoegear for Euston – Watford line services. Class 313/1.

| 313 001 | * | N | NNLX | BY | 62529 71213 62593 |
|---|---|---|---|---|---|
| 313 002 | * | N | NNLX | BY | 62530 71214 62594 |
| 313 003 | * | N | NNLX | BY | 62531 71215 62595 |
| 313 004 | * | N | NNLX | BY | 62532 71216 62596 |
| 313 005 | * | N | NNLX | BY | 62533 71217 62597 |
| 313 006 | * | N | NNLX | BY | 62534 71218 62598 |
| 313 007 | * | N | NNLX | BY | 62535 71219 62599 |
| 313 008 | * | N | NNLX | BY | 62536 71220 62600 |
| 313 009 | * | N | NNLX | BY | 62537 71221 62601 |
| 313 010 | * | N | NNLX | BY | 62538 71222 62602 |
| 313 011 | * | N | NNLX | BY | 62539 71223 62603 |
| 313 012 | * | N | NNLX | BY | 62540 71224 62604 |
| 313 013 | * | N | NNLX | BY | 62541 71225 62605 |
| 313 014 | * | N | NNLX | BY | 62542 71226 62606 |
| 313 015 | * | N | NNLX | BY | 62543 71227 62607 |
| 313 016 | * | N | NNLX | BY | 62544 71228 62608 |
| 313 017 | * | N | NNLX | BY | 62545 71229 62609 |
| 313 018 | * | N | NGNX | HE | 62546 71230 62610 |
| 313 019 | * | N | NGNX | HE | 62547 71231 62611 |
| 313 020 | * | N | NGNX | HE | 62548 71232 62612 |
| 313 021 | * | N | NNLX | BY | 62549 71233 62613 |
| 313 022 | * | N | NNLX | BY | 62550 71234 62614 |
| 313 023 | * | N | NGNX | HE | 62551 71235 62615 |
| 313 024 | | N | NGNX | HE | 62552 71236 62616 |
| 313 025 | | N | NGNX | HE | 62553 71237 62617 |
| 313 026 | | N | NGNX | HE | 62554 71238 62618 |
| 313 027 | | N | NGNX | HE | 62555 71239 62619 |

| 313 028 | N | NGNX | HE | 62556 71240 62620 |
| 313 029 | N | NGNX | HE | 62557 71241 62621 |
| 313 030 | N | NGNX | HE | 62558 71242 62622 |
| 313 031 | N | NGNX | HE | 62559 71243 62623 |
| 313 032 | N | NGNX | HE | 62560 71244 62624 |
| 313 033 | N | NGNX | HE | 62561 71245 62625 |
| 313 034 | N | NGNX | HE | 62562 71246 62626 |
| 313 035 | N | NGNX | HE | 62563 71247 62627 |
| 313 036 | N | NGNX | HE | 62564 71248 62628 |
| 313 037 | N | NGNX | HE | 62565 71249 62629 |
| 313 038 | N | NGNX | HE | 62566 71250 62630 |
| 313 039 | N | NGNX | HE | 62567 71251 62631 |
| 313 040 | N | NGNX | HE | 62568 71252 62632 |
| 313 041 | N | NGNX | HE | 62569 71253 62633 |
| 313 042 | N | NGNX | HE | 62570 71254 62634 |
| 313 043 | N | NGNX | HE | 62571 71255 62635 |
| 313 044 | N | NGNX | HE | 62572 71256 62636 |
| 313 045 | N | NGNX | HE | 62573 71257 62637 |
| 313 046 | N | NGNX | HE | 62574 71258 62638 |
| 313 047 | N | NGNX | HE | 62575 71259 62639 |
| 313 048 | N | NGNX | HE | 62576 71260 62640 |
| 313 049 | N | NGNX | HE | 62577 71261 62641 |
| 313 050 | N | NGNX | HE | 62578 71262 62642 |
| 313 051 | N | NGNX | HE | 62579 71263 62643 |
| 313 052 | N | NGNX | HE | 62580 71264 62644 |
| 313 053 | N | NGNX | HE | 62581 71265 62645 |
| 313 054 | N | NGNX | HE | 62582 71266 62646 |
| 313 055 | N | NGNX | HE | 62583 71267 62647 |
| 313 056 | N | NGNX | HE | 62584 71268 62648 |
| 313 057 | N | NGNX | HE | 62585 71269 62649 |
| 313 058 | N | NGNX | HE | 62586 71270 62650 |
| 313 059 | N | NGNX | HE | 62587 71271 62651 |
| 313 060 | N | NGNX | HE | 62588 71272 62652 |
| 313 061 | N | NGNX | HE | 62589 71273 62653 |
| 313 062 | N | NGNX | HE | 62590 71274 62654 |
| 313 063 | N | NGNX | HE | 62591 71275 62655 |
| 313 064 | N | NGNX | HE | 62592 71276 62656 |

## CLASS 314

DMSO – PTSO – DMSO. Thyristor control. Tightlock couplers. Sliding doors. Disc and rheostatic brakes. PA. Cab to shore radio.
**Bogies:** BX1.
**Gangways:** Within unit. End doors.
**Traction Motors:** Four GEC G310AZ (Brush TM61-53*) of 82.125 kW.
**Dimensions:** 19.80 x 2.82 m (outer cars), 19.92 x 2.82 m (inner cars).
**Maximum Speed:** 75 mph.

**DMSO.** Dia. EA206. Lot No. 30912 York 1979. 68S. 34.5 t.
**PTSO.** Dia. EH211. Lot No. 30913 York 1979. 76S. 33.0 t.

| 314 201 | * | S | RAGW | GW | 64583 71450 64584 |
| 314 202 | * | S | RAGW | GW | 64585 71451 64586 |

| 314 204 | * | S | RAGW | GW | 64589 71453 64590 |
|---|---|---|---|---|---|
| 314 205 | * | S | RAGW | GW | 64591 71454 64592 |
| 314 206 | * | S | RAGW | GW | 64593 71455 64594 |
| 314 207 | | S | RAGW | GW | 64595 71456 64596 |
| 314 208 | | S | RAGW | GW | 64597 71457 64598 |
| 314 209 | | S | RAGW | GW | 64599 71458 64600 |
| 314 210 | | S | RAGW | GW | 64601 71459 64602 |
| 314 211 | | S | RAGW | GW | 64603 71460 64604 |
| 314 212 | | S | RAGW | GW | 64605 71461 64606 |
| 314 213 | | S | RAGW | GW | 64607 71462 64608 |
| 314 214 | | S | RAGW | GW | 64609 71463 64610 |
| 314 215 | | S | RAGW | GW | 64611 71464 64612 |
| 314 216 | | S | RAGW | GW | 64613 71465 64614 |
| Spare | * | S | RAGW | GW (S) | 64587 71452 |

# CLASS 315

DMSO – TSO – PTSO – DMSO. Thyristor control. Tightlock couplers. Sliding doors. Disc and rheostatic brakes. PA.
**Bogies:** BX1.
**Gangways:** Within unit. End doors.
**Traction Motors:** Four Brush TM61-53 (GEC G310AZ*) of 82.125 kW.
**Dimensions:** 19.80 x 2.82 m (outer cars), 19.92 x 2.82 m (inner cars).
**Maximum Speed:** 75 mph.

**64461 – 64582. DMSO.** Dia. EA207. Lot. No. 30902 York 1980 – 81. 74S. 35 t.
**71281 – 71341. TSO.** Dia. EH216. Lot No. 30904 York 1980 – 81. 86S. 25.5 t.
**71389 – 71449. PTSO.** Dia. EH217. Lot No. 30903 York 1980 – 81. 84S. 32 t.

| 315 801 | N | NGEX | IL | 64461 71281 71389 64462 |
|---|---|---|---|---|
| 315 802 | N | NGEX | IL | 64463 71282 71390 64464 |
| 315 803 | N | NGEX | IL | 64465 71283 71391 64466 |
| 315 804 | N | NGEX | IL | 64467 71284 71392 64468 |
| 315 805 | N | NGEX | IL | 64469 71285 71393 64470 |
| 315 806 | N | NGEX | IL | 64471 71286 71394 64472 |
| 315 807 | N | NGEX | IL | 64473 71287 71395 64474 |
| 315 808 | N | NGEX | IL | 64475 71288 71396 64476 |
| 315 809 | N | NGEX | IL | 64477 71289 71397 64478 |
| 315 810 | N | NGEX | IL | 64479 71290 71398 64480 |
| 315 811 | N | NGEX | IL | 64481 71291 71399 64482 |
| 315 812 | N | NGEX | IL | 64483 71292 71400 64484 |
| 315 813 | N | NGEX | IL | 64485 71293 71401 64486 |
| 315 814 | N | NGEX | IL | 64487 71294 71402 64488 |
| 315 815 | N | NGEX | IL | 64489 71295 71403 64490 |
| 315 816 | N | NGEX | IL | 64491 71296 71404 64492 |
| 315 817 | N | NGEX | IL | 64493 71297 71405 64494 |
| 315 818 | N | NGEX | IL | 64495 71298 71406 64496 |
| 315 819 | N | NGEX | IL | 64497 71299 71407 64498 |
| 315 820 | N | NGEX | IL | 64499 71300 71408 64500 |
| 315 821 | N | NGEX | IL | 64501 71301 71409 64502 |
| 315 822 | N | NGEX | IL | 64503 71302 71410 64504 |
| 315 823 | N | NGEX | IL | 64505 71303 71411 64506 |

| 315 824 |   | N | NGEX | IL | 64507 | 71304 | 71412 | 64508 |
| 315 825 |   | N | NGEX | IL | 64509 | 71305 | 71413 | 64510 |
| 315 826 |   | N | NGEX | IL | 64511 | 71306 | 71414 | 64512 |
| 315 827 |   | N | NGEX | IL | 64513 | 71307 | 71415 | 64514 |
| 315 828 |   | N | NGEX | IL | 64515 | 71308 | 71416 | 64516 |
| 315 829 |   | N | NGEX | IL | 64517 | 71309 | 71417 | 64518 |
| 315 830 |   | N | NGEX | IL | 64519 | 71310 | 71418 | 64520 |
| 315 831 |   | N | NGEX | IL | 64521 | 71311 | 71419 | 64522 |
| 315 832 |   | N | NGEX | IL | 64523 | 71312 | 71420 | 64524 |
| 315 833 |   | N | NGEX | IL | 64525 | 71313 | 71421 | 64526 |
| 315 834 |   | N | NGEX | IL | 64527 | 71314 | 71422 | 64528 |
| 315 835 |   | N | NGEX | IL | 64529 | 71315 | 71423 | 64530 |
| 315 836 |   | N | NGEX | IL | 64531 | 71316 | 71424 | 64532 |
| 315 837 |   | N | NGEX | IL | 64533 | 71317 | 71425 | 64534 |
| 315 838 |   | N | NGEX | IL | 64535 | 71318 | 71426 | 64536 |
| 315 839 |   | N | NGEX | IL | 64537 | 71319 | 71427 | 64538 |
| 315 840 |   | N | NGEX | IL | 64539 | 71320 | 71428 | 64540 |
| 315 841 |   | N | NGEX | IL | 64541 | 71321 | 71429 | 64542 |
| 315 842 | * | N | NGEX | IL | 64543 | 71322 | 71430 | 64544 |
| 315 843 | * | N | NGEX | IL | 64545 | 71323 | 71431 | 64546 |
| 315 844 | * | N | NGEX | IL | 64547 | 71324 | 71432 | 64548 |
| 315 845 | * | N | NGEX | IL | 64549 | 71325 | 71433 | 64550 |
| 315 846 | * | N | NGEX | IL | 64551 | 71326 | 71434 | 64552 |
| 315 847 | * | N | NGEX | IL | 64553 | 71327 | 71435 | 64554 |
| 315 848 | * | N | NNEX | IL | 64555 | 71328 | 71436 | 64556 |
| 315 849 | * | N | NNEX | IL | 64557 | 71329 | 71437 | 64558 |
| 315 850 | * | N | NNEX | IL | 64559 | 71330 | 71438 | 64560 |
| 315 851 | * | N | NNEX | IL | 64561 | 71331 | 71439 | 64562 |
| 315 852 | * | N | NNEX | IL | 64563 | 71332 | 71440 | 64564 |
| 315 853 | * | N | NNEX | IL | 64565 | 71333 | 71441 | 64566 |
| 315 854 | * | N | NNEX | IL | 64567 | 71334 | 71442 | 64568 |
| 315 855 | * | N | NNEX | IL | 64569 | 71335 | 71443 | 64570 |
| 315 856 | * | N | NNEX | IL | 64571 | 71336 | 71444 | 64572 |
| 315 857 | * | N | NNEX | IL | 64573 | 71337 | 71445 | 64574 |
| 315 858 | * | N | NNEX | IL | 64575 | 71338 | 71446 | 64576 |
| 315 859 | * | N | NNEX | IL | 64577 | 71339 | 71447 | 64578 |
| 315 860 | * | N | NNEX | IL | 64579 | 71340 | 71448 | 64580 |
| 315 861 | * | N | NNEX | IL | 64581 | 71341 | 71449 | 64582 |

# CLASS 317

DTSO – MSO – TCOL – DTSO. Thyristor control. Tightlock couplers. Sliding doors. Disc brakes. PA.
**Bogies:** BP20 (MSO), BT13 (others).
**Gangways:** Throughout.
**Traction Motors:** Four GEC G315BZ of 247.5 kW.
**Dimensions:** 19.83 x 2.82 m (outer cars), 19.92 x 2.82 m (inner cars).
**Maximum Speed:** 100 mph.

Class 317/1. Pressure ventilated.

**DTSO(A)** Dia. EE216. Lot No. 30955 York 1981 – 82. 74S. 29.44 t.
**MSO.** Dia. EC202. Lot No. 30958 York 1981 – 82. 79S. 49.76 t.

**TCOL.** Dia. EH307. Lot No. 30957 Derby 1981 – 82. 22F 46S 2L. 28.80 t. Controlled emission toilets (but decommisioned).
**DTSO(B)** Dia. EE235 (EE232★). Lot No. 30956 York 1981 – 82. 70S. (71S★). 29.28 t.

| | | | | | | | |
|---|---|---|---|---|---|---|---|
| 317 301 | N | NNEX | HE | 77024 | 62661 | 71577 | 77048 |
| 317 302 | N | NNEX | HE | 77001 | 62662 | 71578 | 77049 |
| 317 303 | N | NNEX | HE | 77002 | 62663 | 71579 | 77050 |
| 317 304 | N | NNEX | HE | 77003 | 62664 | 71580 | 77051 |
| 317 305 | N | NNEX | HE | 77004 | 62665 | 71581 | 77052 |
| 317 306 | N | NNEX | HE | 77005 | 62666 | 71582 | 77053 |
| 317 307 | N | NNEX | HE | 77006 | 62667 | 71583 | 77054 |
| 317 308 | N | NNEX | HE | 77007 | 62668 | 71584 | 77055 |
| 317 309 | N | NNEX | HE | 77008 | 62669 | 71585 | 77056 |
| 317 310 | N | NNEX | HE | 77009 | 62670 | 71586 | 77057 |
| 317 311 | N | NNEX | HE | 77010 | 62671 | 71587 | 77058 |
| 317 312 | N | NNEX | HE | 77011 | 62672 | 71588 | 77059 |
| 317 313 | N | NNEX | HE | 77012 | 62673 | 71589 | 77060 |
| 317 314 | N | NNEX | HE | 77013 | 62674 | 71590 | 77061 |
| 317 315 | N | NNEX | HE | 77014 | 62675 | 71591 | 77062 |
| 317 316 | N | NNEX | HE | 77015 | 62676 | 71592 | 77063 |
| 317 317 | N | NNEX | HE | 77016 | 62677 | 71593 | 77064 |
| 317 318 | N | NNEX | HE | 77017 | 62678 | 71594 | 77065 |
| 317 319 | N | NNEX | HE | 77018 | 62679 | 71595 | 77066 |
| 317 320 | N | NNEX | HE | 77019 | 62680 | 71596 | 77067 |
| 317 321 | N | NNEX | HE | 77020 | 62681 | 71597 | 77068 |
| 317 322 | N | NNEX | HE | 77021 | 62682 | 71598 | 77069 |
| 317 323 | N | NNEX | HE | 77022 | 62683 | 71599 | 77070 |
| 317 324 | N | NGNX | HE | 77023 | 62684 | 71600 | 77071 |
| 317 325 | N | NGNX | HE | 77000 | 62685 | 71601 | 77072 |
| 317 326 | N | NGNX | HE | 77025 | 62686 | 71602 | 77073 |
| 317 327 | N | NGNX | HE | 77026 | 62687 | 71603 | 77074 |
| 317 328 | N | NGNX | HE | 77027 | 62688 | 71604 | 77075 |
| 317 329 | N | NGNX | HE | 77028 | 62689 | 71605 | 77076 |
| 317 330 | N | NGNX | HE | 77029 | 62690 | 71606 | 77077 |
| 317 331 | N | NGNX | HE | 77030 | 62691 | 71607 | 77078 |
| 317 332 | N | NGNX | HE | 77031 | 62692 | 71608 | 77079 |
| 317 333 | N | NGNX | HE | 77032 | 62693 | 71609 | 77080 |
| 317 334 | N | NGNX | HE | 77033 | 62694 | 71610 | 77081 |
| 317 335 | N | NGNX | HE | 77034 | 62695 | 71611 | 77082 |
| 317 336 | N | NGNX | HE | 77035 | 62696 | 71612 | 77083 |
| 317 337 | ★ N | NGNX | HE | 77036 | 62697 | 71613 | 77084 |
| 317 338 | ★ N | NGNX | HE | 77037 | 62698 | 71614 | 77085 |
| 317 339 | ★ N | NGNX | HE | 77038 | 62699 | 71615 | 77086 |
| 317 340 | ★ N | NGNX | HE | 77039 | 62700 | 71616 | 77087 |
| 317 341 | ★ N | NGNX | HE | 77040 | 62701 | 71617 | 77088 |
| 317 342 | ★ N | NGNX | HE | 77041 | 62702 | 71618 | 77089 |
| 317 343 | ★ N | NGNX | HE | 77042 | 62703 | 71619 | 77090 |
| 317 344 | ★ N | NGNX | HE | 77043 | 62704 | 71620 | 77091 |
| 317 345 | ★ N | NGNX | HE | 77044 | 62705 | 71621 | 77092 |
| 317 346 | ★ N | NGNX | HE | 77045 | 62706 | 71622 | 77093 |
| 317 347 | ★ N | NGNX | HE | 77046 | 62707 | 71623 | 77094 |
| 317 348 | ★ N | NGNX | HE | 77047 | 62708 | 71624 | 77095 |

Class 317/2. Convection heating.

**77200 – 19. DTSO(A).** Dia. EE224. Lot No. 30994 York 1985 – 86. 74S. 29.31 t.
**77280 – 83. DTSO(A).** Dia. EE224. Lot No. 31007 York 1987. 74S. 29.31 t.
**62846 – 65. MSO.** Dia. EC205. Lot No. 30996 York 1985 – 86. 79S. 50.08 t.
**62886 – 89. MSO.** Dia. EC205. Lot No. 31009 York 1987. 79S. 50.08 t.
**71734 – 53. TCOL.** Dia. EH308. Lot No. 30997 Yk 1985 – 86. 22F 46S 2L. 28.28 t.
**71762 – 65. TCOL.** Dia. EH308. Lot No. 31010 York 1987. 22F 46S 2L. 28.28 t.
**77220 – 39. DTSO(B).** Dia. EE225. Lot No. 30995 York 1985 – 86. 29.28 t. 71S.
**77284 – 87. DTSO(B).** Dia. EE225. Lot No. 31008 York 1987. 29.28 t. 71S.

| | | | | | | |
|---|---|---|---|---|---|---|
| 317 349 | N | NGNX | HE | 77200 | 62846 | 71734 77220 |
| 317 350 | N | NGNX | HE | 77201 | 62847 | 71735 77221 |
| 317 351 | N | NGNX | HE | 77202 | 62848 | 71736 77222 |
| 317 352 | N | NGNX | HE | 77203 | 62849 | 71739 77223 |
| 317 353 | N | NGNX | HE | 77204 | 62850 | 71738 77224 |
| 317 354 | N | NGNX | HE | 77205 | 62851 | 71737 77225 |
| 317 355 | N | NGNX | HE | 77206 | 62852 | 71740 77226 |
| 317 356 | N | NGNX | HE | 77207 | 62853 | 71742 77227 |
| 317 357 | N | NGNX | HE | 77208 | 62854 | 71741 77228 |
| 317 358 | N | NGNX | HE | 77209 | 62855 | 71743 77229 |
| 317 359 | N | NGNX | HE | 77210 | 62856 | 71744 77230 |
| 317 360 | N | NGNX | HE | 77211 | 62857 | 71745 77231 |
| 317 361 | N | NGNX | HE | 77212 | 62858 | 71746 77232 |
| 317 362 | N | NGNX | HE | 77213 | 62859 | 71747 77233 |
| 317 363 | N | NGNX | HE | 77214 | 62860 | 71748 77234 |
| 317 364 | N | NGNX | HE | 77215 | 62861 | 71749 77235 |
| 317 365 | N | NNEX | HE | 77216 | 62862 | 71750 77236 |
| 317 366 | N | NNEX | HE | 77217 | 62863 | 71752 77237 |
| 317 367 | N | NNEX | HE | 77218 | 62864 | 71751 77238 |
| 317 368 | N | NNEX | HE | 77219 | 62865 | 71753 77239 |
| 317 369 | N | NNEX | HE | 77280 | 62886 | 71762 77284 |
| 317 370 | N | NNEX | HE | 77281 | 62887 | 71763 77285 |
| 317 371 | N | NNEX | HE | 77282 | 62888 | 71764 77286 |
| 317 372 | N | NNEX | HE | 77283 | 62889 | 71765 77287 |

**Name:** TCOL No. 71746 of set 317 361 is named 'Kings Lynn Festival'.

# CLASS 318

DTSOL – MSO – DTSO. Thyristor control. Tightlock couplers. Sliding doors. Disc brakes. PA. Cab to shore radio.
**Bogies:** BP20 (MSO), BT13 (others).
**Gangways:** Throughout.
**Traction Motors:** Four Brush TM 2141 of 268 kW.
**Dimensions:** 19.83 x 2.82 m (outer cars), 19.92 x 2.82 m (inner cars).
**Maximum Speed:** 90 mph.

**77240 – 59. DTSOL.** Dia. EE227. Lot No. 30999 York 1985 – 86. 66S 1L. 30.01 t.
**77288. DTSOL.** Dia. EE227. Lot No. 31020 York 1986 – 87. 66S 1L. 30.01 t.

**62866 – 85. MSO.** Dia. EC207. Lot No. 30998 York 1985 – 86. 79S. 50.90 t.
**62890. MSO.** Dia. EC207. Lot No. 31019 York 1987. 79S. 50.90 t.
**77260 – 79. DTSO.** Dia. EE228. Lot No. 31000 York 1985 – 86. 71S. 26.60 t.
**77289. DTSO.** Dia. EE228. Lot No. 31021 York 1987. 71S. 26.60 t.

| | | | | | | |
|---|---|---|---|---|---|---|
| 318 250 | S | RAGW | GW | 77260 | 62866 | 77240 |
| 318 251 | S | RAGW | GW | 77261 | 62867 | 77241 |
| 318 252 | S | RAGW | GW | 77262 | 62868 | 77242 |
| 318 253 | S | RAGW | GW | 77263 | 62869 | 77243 |
| 318 254 | S | RAGW | GW | 77264 | 62870 | 77244 |
| 318 255 | S | RAGW | GW | 77265 | 62871 | 77245 |
| 318 256 | S | RAGW | GW | 77266 | 62872 | 77246 |
| 318 257 | S | RAGW | GW | 77267 | 62873 | 77247 |
| 318 258 | S | RAGW | GW | 77268 | 62874 | 77248 |
| 318 259 | S | RAGW | GW | 77269 | 62875 | 77249 |
| 318 260 | S | RAGW | GW | 77270 | 62876 | 77250 |
| 318 261 | S | RAGW | GW | 77271 | 62877 | 77251 |
| 318 262 | S | RAGW | GW | 77272 | 62878 | 77252 |
| 318 263 | S | RAGW | GW | 77273 | 62879 | 77253 |
| 318 264 | S | RAGW | GW | 77274 | 62880 | 77254 |
| 318 265 | S | RAGW | GW | 77275 | 62881 | 77255 |
| 318 266 | S | RAGW | GW | 77276 | 62882 | 77256 |
| 318 267 | S | RAGW | GW | 77277 | 62883 | 77257 |
| 318 268 | S | RAGW | GW | 77278 | 62884 | 77258 |
| 318 269 | S | RAGW | GW | 77279 | 62885 | 77259 |
| 318 270 | S | RAGW | GW | 77289 | 62890 | 77288 |

**Name:** DTSOL No. 77240 of set 318 250 is named 'GEOFF SHAW'.

# CLASS 319

Thyristor control. Tightlock couplers. Sliding doors. Disc brakes. PA. Cab to shore radio.
**System:** 25 kV a.c. overhead/750 V d.c. third rail.
**Bogies:** P7-4 (MSO), T3-7 (others).
**Gangways:** Within unit. End doors.
**Traction Motors:** Four GEC G315BZ of 247.5 kW.
**Dimensions:** 19.83 x 2.82 m (outer cars), 19.92 x 2.82 m (inner cars).
**Maximum Speed:** 100 mph.

Class 319/0. DTSO – MSO – TSOL – DTSO.

**77291 – 381. DTSO.** Dia. EE233. Lot No. 31022 (odd nos.) York 1987 – 8. 82S. 30 t.
**77431 – 457. DTSO.** Dia. EE233. Lot No. 31038 (odd nos.) York 1988. 82S. 30 t.
**62891 – 936. MSO.** Dia. EC209. Lot No. 31023 York 1987 – 8. 82S. 51 t.
**62961 – 974. MSO.** Dia. EC209. Lot No. 31039 York 1988. 82S. 51 t.
**71772 – 817. TSOL.** Dia. EH234. Lot No. 31024 York 1987 – 8. 77S 2L. 51 t.
**71866 – 879. TSOL.** Dia. EH234. Lot No. 31040 York 1988. 77S 2L. 51 t.
**77290 – 380. DTSO.** Dia. EE234. Lot No. 31025 (even nos.) York 1987 – 8. 78S. 30 t.
**77430 – 456. DTSO.** Dia. EE234. Lot No. 31041 (even nos.) York 1988. 78S. 30 t.

| | | | | | | | |
|---|---|---|---|---|---|---|---|
| 319 001 | N | NSLX | SU | 77291 | 62891 | 71772 | 77290 |
| 319 002 | N | NSLX | SU | 77293 | 62892 | 71773 | 77292 |
| 319 003 | N | NSLX | SU | 77295 | 62893 | 71774 | 77294 |
| 319 004 | N | NSLX | SU | 77297 | 62894 | 71775 | 77296 |
| 319 005 | N | NSLX | SU | 77299 | 62895 | 71776 | 77298 |
| 319 006 | N | NSLX | SU | 77301 | 62896 | 71777 | 77300 |
| 319 007 | N | NSLX | SU | 77303 | 62897 | 71778 | 77302 |
| 319 008 | N | NSLX | SU | 77305 | 62898 | 71779 | 77304 |
| 319 009 | N | NSLX | SU | 77307 | 62899 | 71780 | 77306 |
| 319 010 | N | NSLX | SU | 77309 | 62900 | 71781 | 77308 |
| 319 011 | N | NSLX | SU | 77311 | 62901 | 71782 | 77310 |
| 319 012 | N | NSLX | SU | 77313 | 62902 | 71783 | 77312 |
| 319 013 | N | NSLX | SU | 77315 | 62903 | 71784 | 77314 |
| 319 014 | N | NSLX | SU | 77317 | 62904 | 71785 | 77316 |
| 319 015 | N | NSLX | SU | 77319 | 62905 | 71786 | 77318 |
| 319 016 | N | NSLX | SU | 77321 | 62906 | 71787 | 77320 |
| 319 017 | N | NSLX | SU | 77323 | 62907 | 71788 | 77322 |
| 319 018 | N | NMLX | SU | 77325 | 62908 | 71789 | 77324 |
| 319 019 | N | NMLX | SU | 77327 | 62909 | 71790 | 77326 |
| 319 020 | N | NMLX | SU | 77329 | 62910 | 71791 | 77328 |
| 319 021 | N | NMLX | SU | 77331 | 62911 | 71792 | 77330 |
| 319 022 | N | NMLX | SU | 77333 | 62912 | 71793 | 77332 |
| 319 023 | N | NMLX | SU | 77335 | 62913 | 71794 | 77334 |
| 319 024 | N | NMLX | SU | 77337 | 62914 | 71795 | 77336 |
| 319 025 | N | NMLX | SU | 77339 | 62915 | 71796 | 77338 |
| 319 026 | N | NMLX | SU | 77341 | 62916 | 71797 | 77340 |
| 319 027 | N | NMLX | SU | 77343 | 62917 | 71798 | 77342 |
| 319 028 | N | NMLX | SU | 77345 | 62918 | 71799 | 77344 |
| 319 029 | N | NMLX | SU | 77347 | 62919 | 71800 | 77346 |
| 319 030 | N | NMLX | SU | 77349 | 62920 | 71801 | 77348 |
| 319 031 | N | NMLX | SU | 77351 | 62921 | 71802 | 77350 |
| 319 032 | N | NMLX | SU | 77353 | 62922 | 71803 | 77352 |
| 319 033 | N | NMLX | SU | 77355 | 62923 | 71804 | 77354 |
| 319 034 | N | NMLX | SU | 77357 | 62924 | 71805 | 77356 |
| 319 035 | N | NMLX | SU | 77359 | 62925 | 71806 | 77358 |
| 319 036 | N | NMLX | SU | 77361 | 62926 | 71807 | 77360 |
| 319 037 | N | NMLX | SU | 77363 | 62927 | 71808 | 77362 |
| 319 038 | N | NMLX | SU | 77365 | 62928 | 71809 | 77364 |
| 319 039 | N | NMLX | SU | 77367 | 62929 | 71810 | 77366 |
| 319 040 | N | NMLX | SU | 77369 | 62930 | 71811 | 77368 |
| 319 041 | N | NMLX | SU | 77371 | 62931 | 71812 | 77370 |
| 319 042 | N | NMLX | SU | 77373 | 62932 | 71813 | 77372 |
| 319 043 | N | NMLX | SU | 77375 | 62933 | 71814 | 77374 |
| 319 044 | N | NMLX | SU | 77377 | 62934 | 71815 | 77376 |
| 319 045 | N | NMLX | SU | 77379 | 62935 | 71816 | 77378 |
| 319 046 | N | NMLX | SU | 77381 | 62936 | 71817 | 77380 |
| 319 047 | N | NMLX | SU | 77431 | 62961 | 71866 | 77430 |
| 319 048 | N | NMLX | SU | 77433 | 62962 | 71867 | 77432 |
| 319 049 | N | NMLX | SU | 77435 | 62963 | 71868 | 77434 |
| 319 050 | N | NMLX | SU | 77437 | 62964 | 71869 | 77436 |
| 319 051 | N | NMLX | SU | 77439 | 62965 | 71870 | 77438 |
| 319 052 | N | NMLX | SU | 77441 | 62966 | 71871 | 77440 |

| | | | | |
|---|---|---|---|---|
| 319 053 | N | NMLX | SU | 77443 62967 71872 77442 |
| 319 054 | N | NMLX | SU | 77445 62968 71873 77444 |
| 319 055 | N | NMLX | SU | 77447 62969 71874 77446 |
| 319 056 | N | NMLX | SU | 77449 62970 71875 77448 |
| 319 057 | N | NMLX | SU | 77451 62971 71876 77450 |
| 319 058 | N | NMLX | SU | 77453 62972 71877 77452 |
| 319 059 | N | NMLX | SU | 77455 62973 71878 77454 |
| 319 060 | N | NMLX | SU | 77457 62974 71879 77456 |

Class 319/1. DTCO – MSO – TSOL – DTSO.

**DTCO.** Dia. EE310. Lot No. 31063 York 1990. 16F 54S. 29 t.
**MSO.** Dia. EC214. Lot No. 31064 York 1990. 79S. 50.6 t.
**TSOL.** Dia. EH238. Lot No. 31065 York 1990. 74S 2L. 31 t.
**DTSO.** Dia. EE240. Lot No. 31066 York 1990. 78S. 29.7 t.

| | | | | |
|---|---|---|---|---|
| 319 161 | N | NMLX | SU | 77459 63043 71929 77458 |
| 319 162 | N | NMLX | SU | 77461 63044 71930 77460 |
| 319 163 | N | NMLX | SU | 77463 63045 71931 77462 |
| 319 164 | N | NMLX | SU | 77465 63046 71932 77464 |
| 319 165 | N | NMLX | SU | 77467 63047 71933 77466 |
| 319 166 | N | NMLX | SU | 77469 63048 71934 77468 |
| 319 167 | N | NMLX | SU | 77471 63049 71935 77470 |
| 319 168 | N | NMLX | SU | 77473 63050 71936 77472 |
| 319 169 | N | NMLX | SU | 77475 63051 71937 77474 |
| 319 170 | N | NMLX | SU | 77477 63052 71938 77476 |
| 319 171 | N | NMLX | SU | 77479 63053 71939 77478 |
| 319 172 | N | NMLX | SU | 77481 63054 71940 77480 |
| 319 173 | N | NMLX | SU | 77483 63055 71941 77482 |
| 319 174 | N | NMLX | SU | 77485 63056 71942 77484 |
| 319 175 | N | NMLX | SU | 77487 63057 71943 77486 |
| 319 176 | N | NMLX | SU | 77489 63058 71944 77488 |
| 319 177 | N | NMLX | SU | 77491 63059 71945 77490 |
| 319 178 | N | NMLX | SU | 77493 63060 71946 77492 |
| 319 179 | N | NMLX | SU | 77495 63061 71947 77494 |
| 319 180 | N | NMLX | SU | 77497 63062 71948 77496 |
| 319 181 | N | NMLX | SU | 77973 63093 71979 77974 |
| 319 182 | N | NMLX | SU | 77975 63094 71980 77976 |
| 319 183 | N | NMLX | SU | 77977 63095 71981 77978 |
| 319 184 | N | NMLX | SU | 77979 63096 71982 77980 |
| 319 185 | N | NMLX | SU | 77981 63097 71983 77982 |
| 319 186 | N | NMLX | SU | 77983 63098 71984 77984 |

# CLASS 320

DTSO – MSO – DTSO. Thyristor control. Tightlock couplers. Sliding doors. Disc brakes. PA. New units under construction for Sc.R.
**Bogies:** P7-4 (MSO), T3-7 (others).
**Gangways:** Within unit.
**Traction Motors:** Brush TM2141B of 268 kW.
**Dimensions:** 19.83 x 2.82 m (outer cars), 19.92 x 2.82 m (inner car).
**Maximum Speed:** 75 mph.

**DTSO (A).** Dia. EE238. Lot No. 31060 York 1990. 77S. 30.7 t.

**MSO.** Dia. EC212. Lot No. 31062 York 1990. 77S. 52.1 t.
**DTSO (B).** Dia. EE239. Lot No. 31061 York 1990. 76S 31.7 t.

| 320 301 | S | RAGW | GW | 77899 63021 77921 |
|---------|---|------|----|----|
| 320 302 | S | RAGW | GW | 77900 63022 77922 |
| 320 303 | S | RAGW | GW | 77901 63023 77923 |
| 320 304 | S | RAGW | GW | 77902 63024 77924 |
| 320 305 | S | RAGW | GW | 77903 63025 77925 |
| 320 306 | S | RAGW | GW | 77904 63026 77926 |
| 320 307 | S | RAGW | GW | 77905 63027 77927 |
| 320 308 | S | RAGW | GW | 77906 63028 77928 |
| 320 309 | S | RAGW | GW | 77907 63029 77929 |
| 320 310 | S | RAGW | GW | 77908 63030 77930 |
| 320 311 | S | RAGW | GW | 77909 63031 77931 |
| 320 312 | S | RAGW | GW | 77910 63032 77932 |
| 320 313 | S | RAGW | GW | 77911 63033 77933 |
| 320 314 | S | RAGW | GW | 77912 63034 77934 |
| 320 315 | S | RAGW | GW | 77913 63035 77935 |
| 320 316 | S | RAGW | GW | 77914 63036 77936 |
| 320 317 | S | RAGW | GW | 77915 63037 77937 |
| 320 318 | S | RAGW | GW | 77916 63038 77938 |
| 320 319 | S | RAGW | GW | 77917 63039 77939 |
| 320 320 | S | RAGW | GW | 77918 63040 77940 |
| 320 321 | S | RAGW | GW | 77919 63041 77941 |
| 320 322 | S | RAGW | GW | 77920 63042 77942 |

# CLASS 321

DTCO (DTSO on Class 321/9) – MSO – TSOL – DTSO. Thyristor control. Tightlock couplers. Sliding doors. Disc brakes. PA.
**Bogies:** P7-4 (MSO), T3-7 (others).
**Gangways:** Within unit.
**Traction Motors:** Brush TM2141B (268 kW).
**Dimensions:** 19.83 x 2.82 m (outer cars), 19.92 x 2.82 m (inner cars).
**Maximum Speed:** 100 mph.

Note: Lot numbers and diagrams were officially changed on 09/02/90.

**Class 321/3.** Units built for Liverpool Street workings.

**DTCO.** Dia. EE308. Lot No. 31053 York 1988 – 90. 12F 56S. 29.3 t.
**MSO.** Dia. EC210. Lot No. 31054 York 1988 – 90. 79S. 51.5 t.
**TSOL.** Dia. EH235. Lot No. 31055 York 1988 – 90. 74S 2L. 28 t.
**DTSO.** Dia. EE236. Lot No. 31056 York 1988 – 90. 78S. 29.1 t.

| 321 301 | N | NGEX | IL | 78049 62975 71880 77853 |
|---------|---|------|----|----|
| 321 302 | N | NGEX | IL | 78050 62976 71881 77854 |
| 321 303 | N | NGEX | IL | 78051 62977 71882 77855 |
| 321 304 | N | NGEX | IL | 78052 62978 71883 77856 |
| 321 305 | N | NGEX | IL | 78053 62979 71884 77857 |
| 321 306 | N | NGEX | IL | 78054 62980 71885 77858 |
| 321 307 | N | NGEX | IL | 78055 62981 71886 77859 |
| 321 308 | N | NGEX | IL | 78056 62982 71887 77860 |
| 321 309 | N | NGEX | IL | 78057 62983 71888 77861 |
| 321 310 | N | NGEX | IL | 78058 62984 71889 77862 |

| 321 311 | N | NGEX | IL | 78059 62985 71890 77863 |
| 321 312 | N | NGEX | IL | 78060 62986 71891 77864 |
| 321 313 | N | NGEX | IL | 78061 62987 71892 77865 |
| 321 314 | N | NGEX | IL | 78062 62988 71893 77866 |
| 321 315 | N | NGEX | IL | 78063 62989 71894 77867 |
| 321 316 | N | NGEX | IL | 78064 62990 71895 77868 |
| 321 317 | N | NGEX | IL | 78065 62991 71896 77869 |
| 321 318 | N | NGEX | IL | 78066 62992 71897 77870 |
| 321 319 | N | NGEX | IL | 78067 62993 71898 77871 |
| 321 320 | N | NGEX | IL | 78068 62994 71899 77872 |
| 321 321 | N | NGEX | IL | 78069 62995 71900 77873 |
| 321 322 | N | NGEX | IL | 78070 62996 71901 77874 |
| 321 323 | N | NGEX | IL | 78071 62997 71902 77875 |
| 321 324 | N | NGEX | IL | 78072 62998 71903 77876 |
| 321 325 | N | NGEX | IL | 78073 62999 71904 77877 |
| 321 326 | N | NGEX | IL | 78074 63000 71905 77878 |
| 321 327 | N | NGEX | IL | 78075 63001 71906 77879 |
| 321 328 | N | NGEX | IL | 78076 63002 71907 77880 |
| 321 329 | N | NGEX | IL | 78077 63003 71908 77881 |
| 321 330 | N | NGEX | IL | 78078 63004 71909 77882 |
| 321 331 | N | NGEX | IL | 78079 63005 71910 77883 |
| 321 332 | N | NGEX | IL | 78080 63006 71911 77884 |
| 321 333 | N | NGEX | IL | 78081 63007 71912 77885 |
| 321 334 | N | NGEX | IL | 78082 63008 71913 77886 |
| 321 335 | N | NGEX | IL | 78083 63009 71914 77887 |
| 321 336 | N | NGEX | IL | 78084 63010 71915 77888 |
| 321 337 | N | NGEX | IL | 78085 63011 71916 77889 |
| 321 338 | N | NGEX | IL | 78086 63012 71917 77890 |
| 321 339 | N | NGEX | IL | 78087 63013 71918 77891 |
| 321 340 | N | NGEX | IL | 78088 63014 71919 77892 |
| 321 341 | N | NGEX | IL | 78089 63015 71920 77893 |
| 321 342 | N | NGEX | IL | 78090 63016 71921 77894 |
| 321 343 | N | NGEX | IL | 78091 63017 71922 77895 |
| 321 344 | N | NGEX | IL | 78092 63018 71923 77896 |
| 321 345 | N | NGEX | IL | 78093 63019 71924 77897 |
| 321 346 | N | NGEX | IL | 78094 63020 71925 77898 |
| 321 347 | N | NGEX | IL | 78131 63105 71991 78280 |
| 321 348 | N | NGEX | IL | 78132 63106 71992 78281 |
| 321 349 | N | NGEX | IL | 78133 63107 71993 78282 |
| 321 350 | N | NGEX | IL | 78134 63108 71994 78283 |
| 321 351 | N | NGEX | IL | 78135 63109 71995 78284 |
| 321 352 | N | NGEX | IL | 78136 63110 71996 78285 |
| 321 353 | N | NGEX | IL | 78137 63111 71997 78286 |
| 321 354 | N | NGEX | IL | 78138 63112 71998 78287 |
| 321 355 | N | NGEX | IL | 78139 63113 71999 78288 |
| 321 356 | N | NGEX | IL | 78140 63114 72000 78289 |
| 321 357 | N | NGEX | IL | 78141 63115 72001 78290 |
| 321 358 | N | NGEX | IL | 78142 63116 72002 78291 |
| 321 359 | N | NGEX | IL | 78143 63117 72003 78292 |
| 321 360 | N | NGEX | IL | 78144 63118 72004 78293 |
| 321 361 | N | NGEX | IL | 78145 63119 72005 78294 |
| 321 362 | N | NGEX | IL | 78146 63120 72006 78295 |

| 321 363 | N | NGEX | IL | 78147 63121 72007 78296 |
|---|---|---|---|---|
| 321 364 | N | NGEX | IL | 78148 63122 72008 78297 |
| 321 365 | N | NGEX | IL | 78149 63123 72009 78298 |
| 321 366 | N | NGEX | IL | 78150 63124 72010 78299 |

**Name:** DTSOL No. 71891 of set 321 312 is named 'Southend-on-Sea'.

**Class 321/4.** Units built for WCML workings.

**DTCO.** Dia. EE309. Lot No. 31067 York 1989 – 90. 28F 40S. 29.3 t.
**MSO.** Dia. EC210. Lot No. 31068 York 1989 – 90. 79S. 51.5 t.
**TSOL.** Dia. EH235. Lot No. 31069 York 1989 – 90. 74S 2L. 28 t.
**DTSO.** Dia. EE236. Lot No. 31070 York 1989 – 90. 78S. 29.1 t.

| 321 401 | N | NNWX | BY | 78095 63063 71949 77943 |
|---|---|---|---|---|
| 321 402 | N | NNWX | BY | 78096 63064 71950 77944 |
| 321 403 | N | NNWX | BY | 78097 63065 71951 77945 |
| 321 404 | N | NNWX | BY | 78098 63066 71952 77946 |
| 321 405 | N | NNWX | BY | 78099 63067 71953 77947 |
| 321 406 | N | NNWX | BY | 78100 63068 71954 77948 |
| 321 407 | N | NNWX | BY | 78101 63069 71955 77949 |
| 321 408 | N | NNWX | BY | 78102 63070 71956 77950 |
| 321 409 | N | NNWX | BY | 78103 63071 71957 77951 |
| 321 410 | N | NNWX | BY | 78104 63072 71958 77952 |
| 321 411 | N | NNWX | BY | 78105 63073 71959 77953 |
| 321 412 | N | NNWX | BY | 78106 63074 71960 77954 |
| 321 413 | N | NNWX | BY | 78107 63075 71961 77955 |
| 321 414 | N | NNWX | BY | 78108 63076 71962 77956 |
| 321 415 | N | NNWX | BY | 78109 63077 71963 77957 |
| 321 416 | N | NNWX | BY | 78110 63078 71964 77958 |
| 321 417 | N | NNWX | BY | 78111 63079 71965 77959 |
| 321 418 | N | NNWX | BY | 78112 63080 71966 77960 |
| 321 419 | N | NNWX | BY | 78113 63081 71967 77961 |
| 321 420 | N | NNWX | BY | 78114 63082 71968 77962 |
| 321 421 | N | NNWX | BY | 78115 63083 71969 77963 |
| 321 422 | N | NNWX | BY | 78116 63084 71970 77964 |
| 321 423 | N | NNWX | BY | 78117 63085 71971 77965 |
| 321 424 | N | NNWX | BY | 78118 63086 71972 77966 |
| 321 425 | N | NNWX | BY | 78119 63087 71973 77967 |
| 321 426 | N | NNWX | BY | 78120 63088 71974 77968 |
| 321 427 | N | NNWX | BY | 78121 63089 71975 77969 |
| 321 428 | N | NNWX | BY | 78122 63090 71976 77970 |
| 321 429 | N | NNWX | BY | 78123 63091 71977 77971 |
| 321 430 | N | NNWX | BY | 78124 63092 71978 77972 |
| 321 431 | N | NNWX | BY | 78151 63125 72011 78300 |
| 321 432 | N | NNWX | BY | 78152 63126 72012 78301 |
| 321 433 | N | NNWX | BY | 78153 63127 72013 78302 |
| 321 434 | N | NNWX | BY | 78154 63128 72014 78303 |
| 321 435 | N | NNWX | BY | 78155 63129 72015 78304 |
| 321 436 | N | NNWX | BY | 78156 63130 72016 78305 |
| 321 437 | N | NNWX | BY | 78157 63131 72017 78306 |
| 321 438 | N | NNWX | BY | 78158 63132 72018 78307 |
| 321 439 | N | NNWX | BY | 78159 63133 72019 78308 |
| 321 440 | N | NNWX | BY | 78160 63134 72020 78309 |

| 321 441 | N | NNEX | IL | 78161 63135 72021 78310 |
|---------|---|------|----|---------|
| 321 442 | N | NNEX | IL | 78162 63136 72022 78311 |
| 321 443 | N | NNEX | IL | 78125 63099 71985 78274 |
| 321 444 | N | NNEX | IL | 78126 63100 71986 78275 |
| 321 445 | N | NNEX | IL | 78127 63101 71987 78276 |
| 321 446 | N | NNEX | IL | 78128 63102 71988 78277 |
| 321 447 | N | NNEX | IL | 78129 63103 71989 78278 |
| 321 448 | N | NNEX | IL | 78130 63104 71990 78279 |

**Class 321/9.** West Yorkshire PTE Units. DTSO(A) – MSO – TSOL – DTSO(B).

**DTSO (A).** Dia. EE277. Lot No. 31108 York 1991. 78S. 29.3 t.
**MSO.** Dia. EC216. Lot No. 31109 York 1991. 79S. 51.5 t.
**TSOL.** Dia. EH240. Lot No. 31110 York 1991. 74S 2L. 28 t.
**DTSO (B).** Dia. EE277. Lot No. 31111 York 1991. 78S. 29.1 t.

| 321 901 | Y | RBNL | NL | 77990 63153 72128 77993 |
|---------|---|------|----|---------|
| 321 902 | Y | RBNL | NL | 77991 63154 72129 77994 |
| 321 903 | Y | RBNL | NL | 77992 63155 72130 77995 |

# CLASS 322      STANSTED EXPRESS STOCK

DTCO – MSO – TSOL – DTSO. Units dedicated for use on Stansted Airport services. Thyristor control. Tightlock couplers. Sliding doors. Disc brakes. PA.
**Bogies:** P7-4 (MSO), T3-7 (others).
**Gangways:** Within unit.
**Traction Motors:** Brush TM2141B (268 kW).
**Dimensions:** 19.83 x 2.82 m (outer cars), 19.92 x 2.82 m (inner cars).
**Maximum Speed:** 100 mph.
**Non-Standard Livery:** Light grey with broad green band and narrow white and dark grey bands. White at cantrail level and on outer ends of end cars. 'Stansted Express' lettering.

**DTCO.** Dia. EE313. Lot No. 31094 York 1990. 35F 22S. 30.43 t.
**MSO.** Dia. EC215. Lot No. 31092 York 1990. 70S. 52.27 t.
**TSOL.** Dia. EH239. Lot No. 31093 York 1990. 60S 2L. 29.51 t.
**DTSO.** Dia. EE242. Lot No. 31091 York 1990. 65S. 29.77 t.

| 322 481 | 0 | NNEX | IL | 78163 63137 72023 77985 |
|---------|---|------|----|---------|
| 322 482 | 0 | NNEX | IL | 78164 63138 72024 77986 |
| 322 483 | 0 | NNEX | IL | 78165 63139 72025 77987 |
| 322 484 | 0 | NNEX | IL | 78166 63140 72026 77988 |
| 322 485 | 0 | NNEX | IL | 78167 63141 72027 77989 |

# CLASS 323

DMSO(A) – TSOL – DMSO(B). New units under construction for West Midlands PTE and Greater Manchester PTE areas. Aluminium alloy bodies. Thyristor control. Tightlock couplers. Sliding doors. Disc brakes. PA.
**Bogies:**
**Gangways:** Within unit.
**Traction Motors:**
**Dimensions:**
**Maximum Speed:** 75 mph.

**DMSO(A).** Dia. EA272. Lot No. 31112 Hunslet 1992 – 3. 98S (82S*).   . t.
**TSOL.** Dia. EH296. Lot No. 31113 Hunslet 1992 – 3. 88S 1L. (80S 1L*).   . t.
**DMSO(B).** Dia. EA272. Lot No. 31114 Hunslet 1992 – 3. 98S (82S*).   . t.

| | | | | | |
|---|---|---|---|---|---|
| 323 201 | CE | RDBY | 64001 | 72201 | 65001 |
| 323 202 | CE | RDBY | 64002 | 72202 | 65002 |
| 323 203 | CE | RDBY | 64003 | 72203 | 65003 |
| 323 204 | CE | RDBY | 64004 | 72204 | 65004 |
| 323 205 | CE | RDBY | 64005 | 72205 | 65005 |
| 323 206 | CE | RDBY | 64006 | 72206 | 65006 |
| 323 207 | CE | RDBY | 64007 | 72207 | 65007 |
| 323 208 | CE | RDBY | 64008 | 72208 | 65008 |
| 323 209 | CE | RDBY | 64009 | 72209 | 65009 |
| 323 210 | CE | RDBY | 64010 | 72210 | 65010 |
| 323 211 | CE | RDBY | 64011 | 72211 | 65011 |
| 323 212 | CE | RDBY | 64012 | 72212 | 65012 |
| 323 213 | CE | RDBY | 64013 | 72213 | 65013 |
| 323 214 | CE | RDBY | 64014 | 72214 | 65014 |
| 323 215 | CE | RDBY | 64015 | 72215 | 65015 |
| 323 216 | CE | RDBY | 64016 | 72216 | 65016 |
| 323 217 | CE | RDBY | 64017 | 72217 | 65017 |
| 323 218 | CE | RDBY | 64018 | 72218 | 65018 |
| 323 219 | CE | RDBY | 64019 | 72219 | 65019 |
| 323 220 | CE | RDBY | 64020 | 72220 | 65020 |
| 323 221 | CE | RDBY | 64021 | 72221 | 65021 |
| 323 222 | CE | RDBY | 64022 | 72222 | 65022 |
| 323 223 | * GM | RCLG | 64023 | 72223 | 65023 |
| 323 224 | * GM | RCLG | 64024 | 72224 | 65024 |
| 323 225 | * GM | RCLG | 64025 | 72225 | 65025 |
| 323 226 | GM | RCLG | 64026 | 72226 | 65026 |
| 323 227 | GM | RCLG | 64027 | 72227 | 65027 |
| 323 228 | GM | RCLG | 64028 | 72228 | 65028 |
| 323 229 | GM | RCLG | 64029 | 72229 | 65029 |
| 323 230 | GM | RCLG | 64030 | 72230 | 65030 |
| 323 231 | GM | RCLG | 64031 | 72231 | 65031 |
| 323 232 | GM | RCLG | 64032 | 72232 | 65032 |
| 323 233 | GM | RCLG | 64033 | 72233 | 65033 |
| 323 234 | GM | RCLG | 64034 | 72234 | 65034 |
| 323 235 | GM | RCLG | 64035 | 72235 | 65035 |
| 323 236 | GM | RCLG | 64036 | 72236 | 65036 |
| 323 237 | GM | RCLG | 64037 | 72237 | 65037 |
| 323 238 | GM | RCLG | 64038 | 72238 | 65038 |
| 323 239 | GM | RCLG | 64039 | 72239 | 65039 |

# SOUTHERN REGION 750 V d.c. EMUs

These classes are all allocated to the Southern Region and operate on the third rail system at 750 – 850 V d.c. Except where stated otherwise, all multiple units can run in multiple with one another. Buffet cars have electric cooking. In addition to the class number, the old SR designations e.g. 2 Hap are quoted together with the year of introduction of their type of control gear. Whilst outer couplings are buckeyes on all units, 1951 and 1957-type suburban units have centre buffers and three link couplings within a unit.

## CLASS 438                                                    4 TC

DTSO – TFK – TBSK – DTSO or DTSO – TBSK – DTSO. Converted from loco-hauled stock. Unpowered units which worked push & pull with class 431/2 tractor units and class 33/1 and 73 locos. Express stock. Two units remain and have regained their original numbers for use on charter and special services.

**Electrical Equipment:** 1966-type.
**Bogies:** B5 (SR) bogies.
**Gangways:** Throughout.
**Dimensions:** 19.66 x 2.82 m.
**q1ximum Speed:** 90 mph.

**DTSO.** Dia. EE266. Lot No. 30764 York 1966 – 67. 64S. 32 t.
**TCK.** Dia. EH363. Lot No. 30766 York 1966 – 67. 42F 2L. 33.5 t.
**70812 – 70843. TBSK.** Dia. EJ260. Lot No. 30765 York 1966 – 67. 32S 1L. 35.5 t.
**TBSK.** Dia. EJ260. Lot No. 30855 York 1974. 32S 1L. 35.5 t.

Renumbered from 8010/8017. Formerly class 491.

| 410 | (8010) | pa **B** | NSSX | BM | 76288 | 70859 | 70812 | 76287 |
| 417 | (8017) | pa **B** | NSSX | BM | 76302 | 70860 | 70826 | 76301 |
| Spare | | **N** | NSSX | BM (S) | | | | 76275 |

**Former numbers of vehicles converted from hauled stock:**

| | | | |
|---|---|---|---|
| 70812 (34987) | 70860 (13019) | 76287 ( 4379) | 76301 ( 4375) |
| 70826 (34980) | 76275 ( 3929) | 76288 ( 4391) | 76302 ( 4382) |
| 70859 (13040) | | | |

## CLASS 421/1                                          4 Cig (PHASE 1)

DTCsoL (A) – MBSO – TSO – DTCsoL (B). Express stock. Fitted with electric parking brake.

**Electrical Equipment:** 1963-type.
**Bogies:** Two Mk. 4 motor bogies (MBSO). B5 (SR) bogies (trailer cars).
**Gangways:** Throughout.
**Traction Motors:** Four EE507 of 185 kW.
**Dimensions:** 19.75 x 2.82 m.
**Maximum Speed:** 90 mph.

**DTCsoL(A).** Dia. EE364. Lot No. 30741 York 1964 – 65. 18F 36S 2L. 35.5 t.
**MBSO.** Dia. ED260. Lot No. 30742 York 1964 – 65. 56S. 49 t.
**TSO.** Dia. EH275. Lot No. 30730 York 1964 – 65. 72S. 31.5 t.

DTCsoL(B). Dia. EE363. Lot No. 30740 York 1964–65. 24F 28S 2L.

Renumbered from 7327.

| 1127 | N | NSXX | Bl | 76102 62043 70721 76048 |

# CLASS 421       4 Cig (PHASE 2)

Summary of Lot Numbers.

**76561–76570. DTCsoL(A).** Lot No. 30802 York 1970. 18F 36S 2L. 35.5 t.
**76581–76610. DTCsoL(A).** Lot No. 30806 York 1970. 18F 36S 2L. 35.5 t.
**76717–76787. DTCsoL(A).** Lot No. 30814 York 1970–72. 18F 36S 2L. 35.5 t.
**76859. DTCsoL(A).** Lot No. 30827 York 1972. 18F 36S 2L. 35.5 t.
**62277–62286. MBSO.** Lot No. 30804 York 1970. 56S. 49t.
**62287–62316. MBSO.** Lot No. 30808 York 1970. 56S. 49t.
**62315–62425. MBSO.** Lot No. 30816 York 1970. 56S. 49t.
**62430. MBSO.** Lot No. 30829 York 1972. 56S. 49t.
**70967–70996. TSO.** Lot No. 30809 York 1970–71. 72S. 31.5t.
**71035–71105. TSO.** Lot No. 30817 York 1970. 72S. 31.5t.
**71106. TSO.** Lot No. 30830 York 1972. 72S. 31.5t.
**71926–71928. TSO.** Lot No. 30805 York 1970. 72S. 31.5t.
**76571–76580. DTCsoL(B).** Lot No. 30802 York 1970. 24F 28S 2L. 35 t.
**76611–76640. DTCsoL(B).** Lot No. 30807 York 1970. 24F 28S 2L. 35 t.
**76788–76858. DTCsoL(B).** Lot No. 30815 York 1970–72. 24F 28S 2L. 35 t.
**76859. DTCsoL(B).** Lot No. 30828 York 1972. 24F 28S 2L. 35 t.

Note: DTCsoL(B) seat 18F 36S 2L in refurbished units.

# CLASS 421/2       4 Cig (PHASE 2)

DTCsoL (A)–MBSO–TSO–DTCsoL (B). Express stock.

**Diagram Numbers:** EE364, ED260, EH275, EE363.
**Electrical Equipment:** 1963-type.
**Bogies:** Two Mk. 6 motor bogies (MBSO). B5 (SR) bogies (trailer cars).
**Gangways:** Throughout.
**Traction Motors:** Four EE507 of 185 kW.
**Dimensions:** 19.75 x 2.82 m.
**Maximum Speed:** 90 mph.

Renumbered from the series 7401–7426.

| 1216 | N | NSSX | EH | 76766 62404 71084 76837 |
| 1223 | N | NSSX | EH | 76773 62411 71091 76844 |
| 1224 | N | NSSX | EH | 76774 62412 71092 76845 |
| 1225 | N | NSSX | EH | 76775 62413 71093 76846 |
| 1226 | N | NSSX | EH | 76776 62414 71094 76847 |

# CLASS 421/5    'GREYHOUND' 4 Cig (PHASE 2)

DTCsoL–MBSO–TSO–DTCsoL. Express stock. Facelifted with new trim, fluorescent lighting in saloons, PA. Fitted with an additional stage of field weakening to improve the maximum attainable speed.

**Diagram Numbers:** EE369, ED264, EH287, EE369.

**Electrical Equipment:** 1963-type.
**Bogies:** Two Mk. 6 motor bogies (MBSO). B5 (SR) bogies (trailer cars).
**Gangways:** Throughout.
**Traction Motors:** Four EE507 of 185 kW.
**Dimensions:** 19.75 x 2.82 m.
**Maximum Speed:** 90 mph.

| | | | | | | | |
|---|---|---|---|---|---|---|---|
| 1301 | (1814) | N | NSSX | EH | 76595 62301 70981 76625 | | |
| 1302 | (1815) | N | NSSX | EH | 76584 62290 70970 76614 | | |
| 1303 | (1816) | N | NSSX | EH | 76581 62287 70967 76611 | | |
| 1304 | (1817) | N | NSSX | EH | 76583 62289 70969 76613 | | |
| 1305 | (1818) | N | NSSX | EH | 76717 62355 71035 76788 | | |
| 1306 | (1819) | N | NSSX | EH | 76723 62361 71041 76794 | | |
| 1307 | (1820) | N | NSSX | EH | 76586 62292 70972 76616 | | |
| 1308 | (1821) | N | NSSX | EH | 76627 62298 70978 76622 | | |
| 1309 | (1822) | N | NSSX | EH | 76594 62300 70980 76624 | | |
| 1310 | (1823) | N | NSSX | EH | 76567 62283 71926 76577 | | |
| 1311 | (1824) | N | NSSX | EH | 76561 62277 71927 76571 | | |
| 1312 | (1825) | N | NSSX | EH | 76562 62278 71928 76572 | | |
| 1313 | (1252) | N | NSSX | EH | 76596 62302 70982 76626 | | |
| 1314 | (1244) | N | NSSX | EH | 76588 62294 70974 76618 | | |
| 1315 | (1264) | N | NSSX | EH | 76608 62314 70994 76638 | | |
| 1316 | (1241) | N | NSSX | EH | 76585 62291 70971 76615 | | |
| 1317 | (1253) | N | NSSX | EH | 76597 62303 70983 76592 | | |
| 1318 | (1849) | N | NSSX | EH | 76590 62296 70976 76620 | | |
| 1319 | (1852) | N | NSSX | EH | 76591 62297 70977 76621 | | |
| 1320 | (1836) | N | NSSX | EH | 76593 62299 70979 76623 | | |
| 1321 | (1844) | N | NSSX | EH | 76589 62295 70975 76619 | | |
| 1322 | (1838) | N | NSSX | EH | 76587 62293 70973 76617 | | |

Former numbers of converted buffet cars:

71926 (69315)  |71927 (69330)  |71928 (69331)  |

Note: No new Lot Nos were issued for the above conversions.

---

# CLASS 411/4* & 411/5          REFURBISHED 4 Cep

DMSO (A) – TBCK – TSOL – DMSO (B). Kent Coast Express Stock. Refurbished and renumbered from the 71/72xx series. Fitted with hopper ventilators, Inter-City 70 seats, fluorescent lighting and PA.

**Electrical Equipment:** 1957-type (*1951-type).
**Bogies:** One Mk. 4 (Mk 3B§) motor bogie (DMSO). Commonwealth trailer bogies.
**Gangways:** Throughout.
**Traction Motors:** Two EE507 of 185 kW.
**Dimensions:** 19.75 x 2.82 m.
**Maximum Speed:** 90 mph.

★ – 70345 is a TBFK with one compartment declassified. It is from the original refurbished unit (1500), has a different interior colour scheme and does not have hopper ventilators.

61305 has four seats at inner vestibule end replaced by luggage racks.

**DMSO (A).** Dia. EA263. 64S. 44.15 t.
**TBCK. Dia.** EJ361. 24F 6S 2L. 36.17 t.
**TSOL. Dia.** EH282. 64S 2L. 33.78 t.
**DMSO (B).** Dia. EA264. 64S. 43.54 t.

Lot numbers are as follows, all cars being built at Ashford/Eastleigh:

61033 – 61040. Lot No. 30108 1956.
61041 – 61044. Lot No. 30111 1956.
61229 – 61240. Lot No. 30449 1958.
61304 – 61409. Lot No. 30454 1958 – 59.
61694 – 61811. Lot No. 30619 1960 – 61.
61868 – 61870. Lot No. 30638 1960 – 61.
61948 – 61961. Lot No. 30708 1963.
70033 – 70036. Lot No. 30109 1956.
70037 – 70040. Lot No. 30110 1956.
70041 – 70042. Lot No. 30112 1956.

70043 – 70044. Lot No. 30639 1961.
70229 – 70234. Lot No. 30450 1958.
70235 – 70240. Lot No. 30451 1958.
70241. Lot No. 30640 1961.
70260 – 70302. Lot No. 30455 1958 – 59.
70303 – 70355. Lot No. 30456 1958 – 59.
70503 – 70551. Lot No. 30620 1960 – 61.
70552 – 70610. Lot No. 30621 1960 – 61.
70653 – 70659. Lot No. 30709 1963.
70660 – 70666. Lot No. 30710 1963.

| | | | | | | | | |
|---|---|---|---|---|---|---|---|---|
| 1501 | * | N | NKCX | RE | 61041 | 70041 | 70034 | 61042 |
| 1502 | * | N | NKCX | RE | 61040 | 70040 | 70036 | 61039 |
| 1503 | * | N | NKCX | RE | 61033 | 70037 | 70033 | 61034 |
| 1504 | * | N | NKCX | RE | 61043 | 70042 | 71712 | 61037 |
| 1505 | * | N | NKCX | RE | 61044 | 70039 | 70035 | 61038 |
| 1506 | | N | NKCX | RE | 61349 | 70325 | 70282 | 61348 |
| 1507 | | N | NKCX | RE | 61363 | 70332 | 70289 | 61362 |
| 1508 | | N | NKCX | RE | 61305 | 70303 | 70260 | 61304 |
| 1509 | | N | NKCX | RE | 61335 | 70318 | 70275 | 61334 |
| 1510 | | N | NKCX | RE | 61365 | 70333 | 70290 | 61364 |
| 1511 | | N | NKCX | RE | 61367 | 70334 | 70291 | 61366 |
| 1512 | | N | NKCX | RE | 61321 | 70311 | 70268 | 61320 |
| 1513 | | N | NKCX | RE | 61796 | 70321 | 70278 | 61340 |
| 1514 | | N | NKCX | RE | 61327 | 70314 | 70271 | 61326 |
| 1515 | | N | NKCX | RE | 61345 | 70323 | 70280 | 61344 |
| 1516 | | N | NKCX | RE | 61319 | 70310 | 70267 | 61318 |
| 1517 | | N | NKCX | RE | 61317 | 70309 | 70266 | 61316 |
| 1518 | | N | NKCX | RE | 61333 | 70317 | 70274 | 61332 |
| 1519 | | N | NKCX | RE | 61403 | 70352 | 70516 | 61402 |
| 1520 | | N | NKCX | RE | 61343 | 70327 | 70284 | 61380 |
| 1521 | | N | NKCX | RE | 61353 | 70324 | 70281 | 61352 |
| 1522 | | N | NKCX | RE | 61347 | 70341 | 70665 | 61346 |
| 1523 | | N | NKCX | RE | 61383 | 70342 | 70299 | 61382 |
| 1524 | | N | NKCX | RE | 61309 | 70305 | 70262 | 61308 |
| 1525 | | N | NKCX | RE | 61235 | 70238 | 70232 | 61236 |
| 1526 | | N | NKCX | RE | 61239 | 70240 | 70234 | 61240 |
| 1527 | | N | NKCX | RE | 61237 | 70239 | 70233 | 61238 |
| 1528 | | N | NKCX | RE | 61379 | 70340 | 70297 | 61378 |
| 1529 | | N | NKCX | RE | 61355 | 70328 | 70285 | 61354 |
| 1530 | | N | NKCX | RE | 61331 | 70316 | 70273 | 61330 |
| 1531 | | N | NKCX | RE | 61233 | 70237 | 70231 | 61234 |
| 1532 | | N | NKCX | RE | 61391 | 70346 | 71626 | 61390 |
| 1533 | | N | NKCX | RE | 61393 | 70347 | 71627 | 61385 |
| 1534 | | N | NKCX | RE | 61405 | 70353 | 71628 | 61404 |
| 1535 | | N | NKCX | RE | 61397 | 70349 | 71629 | 61396 |

| | | | | | | | |
|---|---|---|---|---|---|---|---|
| 1536 | | N | NKCX | RE | 61399 | 70350 | 71631 | 61398 |
| 1537 | | N | NKCX | RE | 61229 | 70235 | 70229 | 61230 |
| 1538 | | N | NKCX | RE | 61307 | 70304 | 70261 | 61306 |
| 1539 | | N | NKCX | RE | 61401 | 70351 | 71632 | 61400 |
| 1540 | | N | NKCX | RE | 61870 | 70343 | 70300 | 61384 |
| 1541 | | N | NKCX | RE | 61409 | 70355 | 71633 | 61408 |
| 1542 | | N | NKCX | RE | 61395 | 70348 | 71634 | 61394 |
| 1543 | | N | NKCX | RE | 61323 | 70312 | 70269 | 61322 |
| 1544 | | N | NKCX | RE | 61315 | 70308 | 70265 | 61314 |
| 1545 | | N | NKCX | RE | 61359 | 70330 | 70287 | 61358 |
| 1546 | | N | NKCX | RE | 61357 | 70329 | 70286 | 61356 |
| 1547 | ★ | N | NKCX | RE | 61329 | 70345 | 70272 | 61328 |
| 1548 | | N | NKCX | RE | 61375 | 70338 | 70295 | 61374 |
| 1549 | | N | NKCX | RE | 61339 | 70320 | 70277 | 61338 |
| 1550 | | N | NKCX | RE | 61313 | 70307 | 70264 | 61312 |
| 1551 | | N | NKCX | RE | 61325 | 70313 | 70270 | 61324 |
| 1552 | | N | NKCX | RE | 61373 | 70337 | 70294 | 61372 |
| 1553 | | N | NKCX | RE | 61351 | 70306 | 70263 | 61350 |
| 1554 | | N | NKCX | RE | 61369 | 70335 | 70292 | 61368 |
| 1555 | | N | NKCX | RE | 61311 | 70326 | 70283 | 61310 |
| 1556 | | N | NKCX | RE | 61371 | 70336 | 70293 | 61370 |
| 1557 | | N | NKCX | RE | 61337 | 70331 | 70288 | 61360 |
| 1558 | | N | NKCX | RE | 61361 | 70319 | 70276 | 61336 |
| 1559 | | N | NKCX | RE | 61377 | 70339 | 70296 | 61376 |
| 1560 | | N | NKCX | RE | 61387 | 70344 | 70301 | 61386 |
| 1561 | | N | NKCX | RE | 61231 | 70604 | 70230 | 61232 |
| 1562 | | N | NKCX | RE | 61407 | 70236 | 70241 | 61406 |
| 1563 | § | N | NKCX | RE | 61740 | 70575 | 70526 | 61741 |
| 1564 | § | N | NKCX | RE | 61788 | 70599 | 70550 | 61789 |
| 1565 | § | N | NKCX | RE | 61762 | 70586 | 71711 | 61763 |
| 1566 | § | N | NKCX | RE | 61722 | 70566 | 70517 | 61723 |
| 1567 | § | N | NKCX | RE | 61786 | 70598 | 70549 | 61787 |
| 1568 | § | N | NKCX | RE | 61766 | 70588 | 70539 | 61767 |
| 1569 | § | N | NKCX | RE | 61782 | 70596 | 70547 | 61783 |
| 1570 | § | N | NKCX | RE | 61738 | 70574 | 70525 | 61739 |
| 1571 | § | N | NKCX | RE | 61806 | 70608 | 71636 | 61807 |
| 1572 | § | N | NKCX | RE | 61734 | 70572 | 70523 | 61735 |
| 1573 | § | N | NKCX | RE | 61726 | 70568 | 70519 | 61727 |
| 1574 | § | N | NKCX | RE | 61792 | 70601 | 71635 | 61793 |
| 1575 | § | N | NKCX | RE | 61768 | 70583 | 70540 | 61769 |
| 1576 | § | N | NKCX | RE | 61770 | 70590 | 70541 | 61771 |
| 1577 | § | N | NKCX | RE | 61718 | 70564 | 70515 | 61719 |
| 1578 | § | N | NKCX | RE | 61700 | 70555 | 70506 | 61701 |
| 1579 | § | N | NKCX | RE | 61772 | 70591 | 70542 | 61773 |
| 1580 | § | N | NKCX | RE | 61756 | 70589 | 70534 | 61757 |
| 1581 | § | N | NKCX | RE | 61784 | 70597 | 70548 | 61785 |
| 1582 | § | N | NKCX | RE | 61748 | 70603 | 71630 | 61797 |
| 1583 | § | N | NKCX | RE | 61746 | 70578 | 70529 | 61747 |
| 1584 | § | N | NKCX | RE | 61752 | 70581 | 70532 | 61753 |
| 1585 | § | N | NKCX | RE | 61710 | 70560 | 70511 | 61711 |
| 1586 | § | N | NKCX | RE | 61714 | 70562 | 70513 | 61715 |
| 1587 | § | N | NKCX | RE | 61764 | 70587 | 71625 | 61765 |

| | | | | | | | |
|---|---|---|---|---|---|---|---|
| 1588 | § | N | NSSX | BM | 61720 | 70044 | 70520 | 61721 |
| 1589 | § | N | NKCX | RE | 61742 | 70576 | 70527 | 61743 |
| 1590 | § | N | NKCX | RE | 61696 | 70553 | 70504 | 61697 |
| 1591 | § | N | NKCX | RE | 61790 | 70600 | 70551 | 61791 |
| 1592 | § | N | NKCX | RE | 61778 | 70594 | 70545 | 61779 |
| 1593 | § | N | NKCX | RE | 61730 | 70570 | 70521 | 61731 |
| 1594 | § | N | NKCX | RE | 61754 | 70582 | 70533 | 61755 |
| 1595 | § | N | NKCX | RE | 61704 | 70557 | 70508 | 61705 |
| 1596 | § | N | NKCX | RE | 61716 | 70563 | 70514 | 61717 |
| 1597 | § | N | NSSX | BM | 61708 | 70559 | 70510 | 61709 |
| 1598 | § | N | NKCX | RE | 61780 | 70595 | 70546 | 61781 |
| 1599 | § | N | NKCX | RE | 61706 | 70558 | 70509 | 61707 |
| 1600 | § | N | NKCX | RE | 61724 | 70567 | 70518 | 61725 |
| 1601 | § | N | NKCX | RE | 61776 | 70593 | 70544 | 61777 |
| 1602 | § | N | NKCX | RE | 61958 | 70565 | 70279 | 61959 |
| 1603 | § | N | NKCX | RE | 61728 | 70569 | 70298 | 61729 |
| 1604 | § | N | NKCX | RE | 61732 | 70571 | 70522 | 61733 |
| 1605 | § | N | NKCX | RE | 61712 | 70561 | 70512 | 61713 |
| 1606 | § | N | NSSX | BM | 61694 | 70552 | 70503 | 61695 |
| 1607 | § | N | NKCX | RE | 61698 | 70554 | 70505 | 61699 |
| 1608 | § | N | NKCX | RE | 61960 | 70659 | 70666 | 61961 |
| 1609 | § | N | NKCX | RE | 61744 | 70577 | 70528 | 61745 |
| 1610 | § | N | NKCX | RE | 61750 | 70580 | 70531 | 61751 |
| 1611 | § | N | NKCX | RE | 61758 | 70584 | 70537 | 61759 |
| 1612 | § | N | NKCX | RE | 61794 | 70602 | 70535 | 61795 |
| 1613 | § | N | NKCX | RE | 61760 | 70585 | 70536 | 61761 |
| 1614 | § | N | NKCX | RE | 61702 | 70556 | 70507 | 61703 |
| 1615 | § | N | NKCX | RE | 61956 | 70657 | 70664 | 61957 |
| 1616 | § | N | NKCX | RE | 61950 | 70654 | 70543 | 61951 |
| 1617 | § | N | NKCX | RE | 61800 | 70605 | 70661 | 61801 |
| 1618 | § | N | NKCX | RE | 61868 | 70043 | 70663 | 61869 |
| 1619 | § | N | NKCX | RE | 61952 | 70655 | 70662 | 61953 |
| 1620 | § | N | NKCX | RE | 61948 | 70653 | 70660 | 61949 |
| 1621 | § | N | NKCX | RE | 61810 | 70610 | 70524 | 61811 |

Former numbers of converted hauled stock:

| | | | |
|---|---|---|---|
| 71625 (4381) | 71629 (3992) | 71633 (4072) | 71636 (4065) |
| 71626 (3916) | 71630 (3988) | 71634 (4059) | 71711 (3994) |
| 71627 (3921) | 71631 (4436) | 71635 (3990) | 71712 (4062) |
| 71628 (3844) | 71632 (4063) | | |

# CLASS 421/3 & 421/6   FACELIFTED 4 Cig (PHASE 1)

DTCsoL – MBSO – TSO – DTCsoL. Express stock. Fitted with electric parking brake. Facelifted with new trim, fluorescent lighting in saloons, PA.

**Diagram Numbers:** EE369, ED264, EH287, EE369.
**Electrical Equipment:** 1963-type.
**Bogies:** Two Mk. 4 motor bogies (MBSO). B5 (SR) bogies (trailer cars).
**Gangways:** Throughout.
**Traction Motors:** Four EE507 of 185 kW.
**Dimensions:** 19.75 x 2.82 m.

**1701 – 1746**

**Maximum Speed:** 90 mph.

For lot numbers see earlier.

\* Units reformed from Class 422 to enable all Class 422 power cars to have Mk. 6 motor bogies. Phase 1 units with phase 2 TSOs.

| | | | | | | | | | |
|---|---|---|---|---|---|---|---|---|---|
| 1701 | (7312) | | N | NSXX | BI | 76087 | 62028 | 70706 | 76033 |
| 1702 | (7326) | | N | NSXX | BI | 76101 | 62042 | 70720 | 76047 |
| 1703 | (7322) | | N | NSXX | BI | 76097 | 62038 | 70716 | 76043 |
| 1704 | (7317) | | N | NSXX | BI | 76092 | 62033 | 70711 | 76038 |
| 1705 | (7301) | | N | NSXX | BI | 76076 | 62017 | 70695 | 76022 |
| 1706 | (7319) | | N | NSXX | BI | 76094 | 62035 | 70713 | 76040 |
| 1707 | (7309) | | N | NSXX | BI | 76084 | 62025 | 70703 | 76030 |
| 1708 | (7335) | | N | NSXX | BI | 76110 | 62051 | 70729 | 76056 |
| 1709 | (7328) | | N | NSXX | BI | 76103 | 62044 | 70722 | 76049 |
| 1710 | (7303) | | N | NSXX | BI | 76078 | 62019 | 70697 | 76024 |
| 1711 | (7033) | | N | NSXX | BI | 76114 | 62055 | 70698 | 76060 |
| 1712 | (7304) | | N | NSXX | BI | 76079 | 62020 | 70698 | 76025 |
| 1713 | (7047) | | N | NSXX | BI | 76128 | 62069 | 71767 | 76074 |
| 1714 | (7302) | | N | NSXX | BI | 76077 | 62018 | 70696 | 76023 |
| 1715 | (7307) | | N | NSXX | BI | 76082 | 62023 | 70701 | 76028 |
| 1716 | (7325) | | N | NSXX | BI | 76100 | 62041 | 71768 | 76046 |
| 1717 | (7308) | | N | NSXX | BI | 76083 | 62024 | 70702 | 76029 |
| 1718 | (7306) | | N | NSXX | BI | 76081 | 62022 | 70700 | 76027 |
| 1719 | (7035) | | N | NSXX | BI | 76116 | 62057 | 70719 | 76062 |
| 1720 | (7038) | | N | NSXX | BI | 76098 | 62039 | 71769 | 76044 |
| 1721 | (7315) | | N | NSXX | BI | 76090 | 62031 | 70709 | 76036 |
| 1722 | (7331) | | N | NSXX | BI | 76106 | 62047 | 70725 | 76052 |
| 1723 | (7332) | | N | NSXX | BI | 76107 | 62048 | 70726 | 76053 |
| 1724 | (7039) | | N | NSXX | BI | 76120 | 62061 | 71770 | 76066 |
| 1725 | (7313) | | N | NSXX | BI | 76088 | 62029 | 70707 | 76034 |
| 1726 | (7334) | | N | NSXX | BI | 76109 | 62050 | 70728 | 76055 |
| 1727 | (7336) | | N | NSXX | BI | 76111 | 62052 | 70730 | 76057 |
| 1728 | (7324) | | N | NSXX | BI | 76099 | 62040 | 70718 | 76045 |
| 1729 | (7329) | | N | NSXX | BI | 76104 | 62045 | 70723 | 76050 |
| 1730 | (7330) | | N | NSXX | BI | 76105 | 62046 | 70724 | 76113 |
| 1731 | (7320) | | N | NSXX | BI | 76095 | 62036 | 70714 | 76041 |
| 1732 | (7321) | | N | NSXX | BI | 76096 | 62037 | 70715 | 76042 |
| 1733 | (1757) | \* | N | NSXX | BI | 76122 | 62063 | 71047 | 76068 |
| 1734 | (1751) | \* | N | NSXX | BI | 76063 | 62054 | 71044 | 76059 |
| 1735 | (1754) | \* | N | NSXX | BI | 76117 | 62058 | 71050 | 76051 |
| 1736 | (1753) | \* | N | NSXX | BI | 76124 | 62065 | 71052 | 76070 |
| 1737 | (1755) | \* | N | NSXX | BI | 76121 | 62062 | 71058 | 76067 |
| 1738 | (1752) | \* | N | NSXX | BI | 76129 | 62064 | 71046 | 76069 |
| 1739 | (1759) | \* | N | NSXX | BI | 76123 | 62070 | 71066 | 76075 |
| 1740 | (1762) | \* | N | NSXX | BI | 76126 | 62067 | 71097 | 76072 |
| 1741 | (1114) | | N | NSXX | BI | 76089 | 62030 | 70708 | 76035 |
| 1742 | (1111) | | N | NSXX | BI | 76086 | 62027 | 70705 | 76032 |
| 1743 | (1756) | \* | N | NSXX | BI | 76118 | 62059 | 71065 | 76064 |
| 1744 | (1758) | \* | N | NSXX | BI | 76127 | 62068 | 71064 | 76073 |
| 1745 | (1110) | | N | NSXX | BI | 76085 | 62026 | 70704 | 76031 |
| 1746 | (1116) | | N | NSXX | BI | 76091 | 62032 | 70710 | 76037 |

| | | | | | | | | |
|---|---|---|---|---|---|---|---|---|
| 1747 | (1118) | | N | NSXX | BI | 76026 | 62034 | 70712 | 76093 |
| 1748 | (1760) | * | N | NSXX | BI | 76115 | 62056 | 71067 | 76061 |
| 1749 | (1761) | * | N | NSXX | BI | 76112 | 62053 | 71068 | 76058 |
| 1750 | (1105) | | N | NSXX | BI | 76080 | 62021 | 70699 | 76039 |
| 1751 | (1100) | | N | NSXX | BI | 76125 | 62066 | 71051 | 76071 |
| 1752 | (1123) | | N | NSXX | BI | 76119 | 62060 | 70717 | 76065 |
| 1753 | ( ) | | | | | | | | |

Former numbers of converted buffet cars:

| | | | |
|---|---|---|---|
| 71766 (69303) | 71768 (69317) | 71769 (69305) | 71770 (69308) |
| 71767 (69314) | | | |

## CLASS 421/4        FACELIFTED 4 Cig (PHASE 2)

DTCsoL – MBSO – TSO – DTCsoL. Express stock. Facelifted with new trim, fluorescent lighting in saloons, PA.

**Diagram Numbers:** EE369, ED264, EH287, EE369.
**Bogies:** Two Mk. 6 motor bogies (MBSO). B5 (SR) bogies (trailer cars).
**Gangways:** Throughout.
**Traction Motors:** Four EE507 of 185 kW.
**Dimensions:** 19.75 x 2.82 m.
**Maximum Speed:** 90 mph.

| | | | | | | | | |
|---|---|---|---|---|---|---|---|---|
| 1801 | (7427) | N | NSXX | BI | 76777 | 62415 | 71095 | 76848 |
| 1803 | (7430) | N | NSXX | BI | 76780 | 62418 | 71098 | 76851 |
| 1804 | (7428) | N | NSXX | BI | 76778 | 62416 | 71096 | 76849 |
| 1805 | (7432) | N | NSXX | BI | 76782 | 62420 | 71100 | 76853 |
| 1806 | (7433) | N | NKCX | RE | 76783 | 62421 | 71101 | 76854 |
| 1807 | (7434) | N | NKCX | RE | 76784 | 62422 | 71102 | 76855 |
| 1808 | (7435) | N | NKCX | RE | 76785 | 62423 | 71103 | 76856 |
| 1809 | (7436) | N | NKCX | RE | 76786 | 62424 | 71104 | 76857 |
| 1810 | (7437) | N | NKCX | RE | 76787 | 62425 | 71105 | 76858 |
| 1811 | (7431) | N | NKCX | RE | 76781 | 62419 | 71099 | 76852 |
| 1812 | (7407) | N | NKCX | RE | 76757 | 62395 | 71075 | 76828 |
| 1813 | (7438) | N | NKCX | RE | 76859 | 62430 | 71106 | 76860 |
| 1831 | (1254) | N | NSXX | BI | 76598 | 62304 | 70984 | 76628 |
| 1832 | (1269) | N | NSXX | BI | 76719 | 62357 | 71037 | 76790 |
| 1833 | (1238) | N | NSXX | BI | 76582 | 62288 | 70968 | 76612 |
| 1834 | (1258) | N | NSXX | BI | 76566 | 62282 | 70988 | 76576 |
| 1835 | (1257) | N | NSXX | BI | 76601 | 62307 | 70987 | 76631 |
| 1837 | (1272) | N | NSXX | BI | 76722 | 62360 | 71040 | 76793 |
| 1839 | (1263) | N | NKCX | RE | 76607 | 62313 | 70993 | 76637 |
| 1840 | (1274) | N | NKCX | RE | 76724 | 62362 | 71042 | 76795 |
| 1841 | (1259) | N | NKCX | RE | 76603 | 62309 | 70989 | 76633 |
| 1842 | (1275) | N | NKCX | RE | 76725 | 62363 | 71043 | 76796 |
| 1843 | (1281) | N | NKCX | RE | 76731 | 62369 | 71049 | 76802 |
| 1845 | (1255) | N | NSXX | BI | 76599 | 62305 | 70985 | 76629 |
| 1846 | (1287) | N | NSXX | BI | 76737 | 62375 | 71055 | 76808 |
| 1847 | (1256) | N | NSXX | BI | 76600 | 62306 | 70986 | 76630 |
| 1848 | (1261) | N | NSXX | BI | 76605 | 62311 | 70991 | 76635 |
| 1850 | (1268) | N | NSXX | BI | 76718 | 62356 | 71036 | 76789 |
| 1851 | (1271) | N | NSXX | BI | 76721 | 62359 | 71039 | 76792 |

47

| 1853 | (1262) | | N | NSXX | BI | 76606 | 62312 | 70992 | 76636 |
| 1854 | (1288) | | N | NSXX | BI | 76738 | 62376 | 71056 | 76809 |
| 1855 | (1270) | | N | NSXX | BI | 76720 | 62358 | 71038 | 76791 |
| 1856 | (1289) | | N | NSXX | BI | 76739 | 62377 | 71057 | 76810 |
| 1857 | (1266) | | N | NSXX | BI | 76610 | 62316 | 70996 | 76640 |
| 1858 | (1260) | | N | NSXX | BI | 76604 | 62310 | 70990 | 76634 |
| 1859 | (1277) | | N | NSXX | BI | 76727 | 62365 | 71045 | 76798 |
| 1860 | (1202) | | N | NSXX | BI | 76752 | 62390 | 71070 | 76823 |
| 1861 | (1285) | | N | NSXX | BI | 76735 | 62373 | 71053 | 76806 |
| 1862 | (1286) | | N | NSXX | BI | 76736 | 62374 | 71054 | 76807 |
| 1863 | (1292) | | N | NSXX | BI | 76742 | 62380 | 71060 | 76813 |
| 1864 | (1291) | | N | NSXX | BI | 76741 | 62379 | 71059 | 76812 |
| 1865 | (1295) | | N | NSXX | BI | 76745 | 62383 | 71063 | 76639 |
| 1866 | (1293) | | N | NSXX | BI | 76743 | 62381 | 71061 | 76814 |
| 1867 | (1294) | | N | NSXX | BI | 76744 | 62382 | 71062 | 76815 |
| 1868 | (1201) | | N | NSXX | BI | 76751 | 62389 | 71069 | 76822 |
| 1869 | (1203) | | N | NSXX | BI | 76753 | 62391 | 71071 | 76804 |
| 1870 | (1221) | | N | NSSX | EH | 76108 | 62409 | 71089 | 76842 |
| 1871 | (1206) | | N | NSSX | EH | 76756 | 62394 | 71074 | 76827 |
| 1872 | (1208) | 2 | N | NSSX | EH | 76771 | 62396 | 71076 | 76829 |
| 1873 | (1209) | | N | NSSX | EH | 76759 | 62397 | 71077 | 76830 |
| 1874 | (1205) | | N | NSXX | BI | 76755 | 62393 | 71073 | 76826 |
| 1875 | (1204) | | N | NSXX | BI | 76754 | 62392 | 71072 | 76825 |
| 1876 | (1211) | | N | NSSX | EH | 76761 | 62399 | 71079 | 76832 |
| 1877 | (1213) | | N | NSSX | EH | 76763 | 62401 | 71081 | 76834 |
| 1878 | (1218) | | N | NSSX | EH | 76768 | 62406 | 71086 | 76839 |
| 1879 | (1210) | | N | NSSX | EH | 76760 | 62398 | 71078 | 76831 |
| 1880 | (1220) | | N | NSSX | EH | 76770 | 62408 | 71088 | 76841 |
| 1881 | (1212) | | N | NSSX | EH | 76762 | 62400 | 71080 | 76833 |
| 1882 | (1215) | | N | NSSX | EH | 76765 | 62403 | 71083 | 76836 |
| 1883 | (1214) | | N | NSSX | EH | 76764 | 62402 | 71082 | 76835 |
| 1884 | (1217) | | N | NSSX | EH | 76767 | 62405 | 71085 | 76838 |
| 1885 | (1219) | | N | NSSX | EH | 76769 | 62407 | 71087 | 76840 |
| 1886 | (1222) | | N | NSSX | EH | 76772 | 62410 | 71090 | 76843 |
| 1887 | ( ) | | | | | | | | |
| 1888 | ( ) | | | | | | | | |
| 1889 | ( ) | | | | | | | | |
| 1890 | ( ) | | | | | | | | |
| 1891 | ( ) | | | | | | | | |

# CLASS 422/2      4 Big (PHASE 2)

DTCsoL (A) – MBSO – TSRB – DTCsoL (B). Express stock.

**Diagram Numbers:** EE369, ED264, EN260, EE369.
**Electrical Equipment:** 1963-type.
**Bogies:** Two Mk. 6 motor bogies (MBSO). B5 (SR) bogies (trailer cars).
**Gangways:** Throughout.
**Traction Motors:** Four EE507 of 185 kW.
**Dimensions:** 19.75 x 2.82 m.
**Maximum Speed:** 90 mph.

**69332 – 69339. TSRB.** Lot No. 30805 York 1970. 40S. 35 t.

| 2203 | (7051) | N | NSXX | BI | 76563 62279 69332 76573 |
|------|--------|---|------|----|--------------------------|
| 2204 | (7052) | N | NSXX | BI | 76564 62280 69336 76574 |
| 2205 | (7053) | N | NSXX | BI | 76565 62281 69339 76575 |
| 2206 | (7054) | N | NSXX | BI | 76602 62308 69338 76632 |
| 2208 | (7056) | N | NSXX | BI | 76568 62284 69334 76578 |
| 2209 | (7057) | N | NSXX | BI | 76569 62285 69335 76579 |
| 2210 | (7058) | N | NSXX | BI | 76570 62286 69337 76580 |

## CLASS 422/3       Facelifted 4 Big (PHASE 2/1)

DTCsoL (A) – MBSO – TSRB – DTCsoL (B). Express stock. Units reformed from
Class 421 to ensure that all Class 422 power cars have Mk. 6 motor bogies.
Phase 2 units with phase 1 TSRBs (except for 69333 which is a phase 2 TSRB).

**Diagram Numbers:** EE369, ED264, EN260, EE369.
**Electrical Equipment:** 1963-type.
**Bogies:** Two Mk. 6 motor bogies (MBSO). B5 (SR) bogies (trailer cars).
**Gangways:** Throughout.
**Traction Motors:** Four EE507 of 185 kW.
**Dimensions:** 19.75 x 2.82 m.
**Maximum Speed:** 90 mph.

**69301 – 69318.** TSRB. Lot No. 30744 York 1966. 40S. 35 t.
**69333.** TSRB. Lot No. 30805 York 1970. 40S. 35 t.

n Buffet not facelifted.

| 2251 | (1276) | | N | NSXX | BI | 76726 62364 69302 76797 |
|------|--------|---|---|------|----|--------------------------|
| 2252 | (1278) | | N | NSXX | BI | 76728 62366 69312 76799 |
| 2253 | (1284) | | N | NSXX | BI | 76734 62372 69313 76805 |
| 2254 | (1282) | | N | NSXX | BI | 76732 62370 69306 76803 |
| 2255 | (1290) | | N | NSXX | BI | 76740 62378 69310 76811 |
| 2256 | (1297) | | N | NSXX | BI | 76747 62385 69307 76818 |
| 2257 | (1279) | | N | NSXX | BI | 76729 62367 69311 76800 |
| 2258 | (1296) | | N | NSXX | BI | 76746 62384 69316 76817 |
| 2259 | (1298) | | N | NSXX | BI | 76748 62386 69318 76819 |
| 2260 | (1299) | | N | NSXX | BI | 76749 62387 69304 76820 |
| 2261 | (1300) | | N | NSXX | BI | 76750 62388 69301 76821 |
| 2262 | (1802) | n | N | NSXX | BI | 76779 62417 69333 76850 |

## CLASS 412       REFURBISHED 4 Bep

DMSO (A) – TBCK – TRB – DMSO (B). Kent Coast Express Stock. Refurbished
and renumbered from the 70xx series. Fitted with hopper ventilators, Inter-City
70 seats, fluorescent lighting and PA.

**Electrical Equipment:** 1957-type.
**Bogies:** One Mk 3B motor bogie (DMSO). Commonwealth trailer bogies.
§ Rebogied with Mk 6 motor bogies and B5(SR) trailer bogies.
* Rebogied with B5(SR) trailer bogies.
**Gangways:** Throughout.
**Traction Motors:** Four EE507 of 185 kW.
**Dimensions:** 19.75 x 2.82 m.
**Maximum Speed:** 90 mph.

**DMSO (A).** Dia. EA263. 64S. 44.15 t.
**TBCK.** Dia. EJ361. 24F 6S 2L. 36.17 t.
**TRSB.** Dia. EN261. 24S 1L + 9 longitudinal buffet chairs. 35.5 t.
**DMSO (B).** Dia. EA264. 64S. 43.54 t.
Lot numbers are as follows, all cars being built at Ashford/Eastleigh:

| | |
|---|---|
| **61736 – 61809.** Lot No. 30619 1960 – 61. | **70354.** Lot No. 30456 1959. |
| **61954 – 61955.** Lot No. 30708 1963. | **70573 – 70609.** Lot No. 30621 1960 – 61. |
| **69341 – 69347.** Lot No. 30622 1961. | **70656.** Lot No. 30709 1963. |

| | | | | | | | | |
|---|---|---|---|---|---|---|---|---|
| 2301 | (7019) | **N** | NSSX | EH | 61804 | 70607 | 69341 | 61805 |
| 2302 | (7194) | **N** | NSSX | EH | 61774 | 70592 | 69342 | 61775 |
| 2303 | (7208) | **N** | NSSX | EH | 61954 | 70656 | 69347 | 61955 |
| 2304 | (7175) | **N** | NSSX | EH | 61736 | 70573 | 69344 | 61737 |
| 2305 | | **N** | NSSX | EH | 61798 | 70354 | 69345 | 61799 |
| 2306 | (7021) | **N** | NSSX | EH | 61808 | 70609 | 69346 | 61809 |
| 2307 | (7018) | **N** | NSSX | EH | 61802 | 70606 | 69343 | 61803 |

Former numbers of converted buffet cars:

| | | | |
|---|---|---|---|
| 69341 (69014) | 69343 (69018) | 69345 (69013) | 69347 (69015) |
| 69342 (69019) | 69344 (69012) | 69346 (69016) | |

# CLASS 442          WESSEX EXPRESS STOCK

DTFsoL – TSOL(A) – MBRSM – TSOL(B) – DTSOL. New express stock for Waterloo – Bournemouth – Weymouth service. Air conditioned (heat pump system). Power-operated sliding plug doors. PA. Can be hauled and heated by any BR ETH fitted locomotive. Multiple working with class 33/1 and 73 locomotives.

**Electrical Equipment:** 1986-type.
**Bogies:** Mk 6 motor bogies (MBRSM). T4 trailer bogies.
**Gangways:** Throughout.
**Traction Motors:** Four EE546 of 300 kW recovered from class 432.
**Dimensions:** 23.00 x 2.74 m (inner cars), 23.15 x 2.74 m (outer cars).
**Maximum Speed:** 100 mph.

**DTFsoL.** Dia. EE160. Lot No. 31030 Derby 1988 – 89. 50F 1L. (36 in six compartments and 14 2+2 in one saloon). Public Telephone. 39.06 t.
**TSOL (A).** Dia. EH288. Lot No. 31032 Derby 1988 – 89. 80S 2L. 35.26 t.
**MBRSM.** Dia. ED265. Lot No. 31034 Derby 1988 – 89. 14S. 54.10 t.
**TSOL (B).** Dia. EH289. Lot No. 31033 Derby 1988 – 89. 76S 2L + wheelchair space. + 2 tip-up seats. 35.36 t.
**DTSOL.** Dia. EE273. Lot No. 31031 Derby 1988 – 89. 78S 1L. 39.06 t.

| | | | | | | | | |
|---|---|---|---|---|---|---|---|---|
| 2401 | **N** | NSSX | BM | 77382 | 71818 | 62937 | 71842 | 77406 |
| 2402 | **N** | NSSX | BM | 77383 | 71819 | 62938 | 71843 | 77407 |
| 2403 | **N** | NSSX | BM | 77384 | 71820 | 62941 | 71844 | 77408 |
| 2404 | **N** | NSSX | BM | 77385 | 71821 | 62939 | 71845 | 77409 |
| 2405 | **N** | NSSX | BM | 77386 | 71822 | 62944 | 71846 | 77410 |
| 2406 | **N** | NSSX | BM | 77389 | 71823 | 62942 | 71847 | 77411 |
| 2407 | **N** | NSSX | BM | 77388 | 71824 | 62943 | 71848 | 77412 |
| 2408 | **N** | NSSX | BM | 77387 | 71825 | 62945 | 71849 | 77413 |
| 2409 | **N** | NSSX | BM | 77390 | 71826 | 62946 | 71850 | 77414 |
| 2410 | **N** | NSSX | BM | 77391 | 71827 | 62948 | 71851 | 77415 |

| 2411 | N | NSSX | BM | 77392 | 71828 | 62940 | 71858 | 77422 |
| 2412 | N | NSSX | BM | 77393 | 71829 | 62947 | 71853 | 77417 |
| 2413 | N | NSSX | BM | 77394 | 71830 | 62949 | 71854 | 77418 |
| 2414 | N | NSSX | BM | 77395 | 71831 | 62950 | 71855 | 77419 |
| 2415 | N | NSSX | BM | 77396 | 71832 | 62951 | 71856 | 77420 |
| 2416 | N | NSSX | BM | 77397 | 71833 | 62952 | 71857 | 77421 |
| 2417 | N | NSSX | BM | 77398 | 71834 | 62953 | 71852 | 77416 |
| 2418 | N | NSSX | BM | 77399 | 71835 | 62954 | 71859 | 77423 |
| 2419 | N | NSSX | BM | 77400 | 71836 | 62955 | 71860 | 77424 |
| 2420 | N | NSSX | BM | 77401 | 71837 | 62956 | 71861 | 77425 |
| 2421 | N | NSSX | BM | 77402 | 71838 | 62957 | 71862 | 77426 |
| 2422 | N | NSSX | BM | 77403 | 71839 | 62958 | 71863 | 77427 |
| 2423 | N | NSSX | BM | 77404 | 71840 | 62959 | 71864 | 77428 |
| 2424 | N | NSSX | BM | 77405 | 71841 | 62960 | 71865 | 77429 |

Names:

| | |
|---|---|
| 62937 BEAULIEU | 62944 CITY OF PORTSMOUTH |
| 62938 COUNTY OF HAMPSHIRE | 62945 COUNTY OF DORSET |
| 62941 THE NEW FOREST | 62951 MARY ROSE |
| 62942 VICTORY | 62955 BBC SOUTH TODAY |
| 62943 THOMAS HARDY | 62959 COUNTY OF SURREY |

# CLASS 423                                                    4 Vep

DTCsoL – MBSO – TSO – DTCsoL. Outer suburban stock.

**Electrical Equipment:** 1963-type.
**Bogies:** Two Mk. 4 motor bogies (MBSO). B5 (SR) bogies (trailer cars).
**Gangways:** Throughout.
**Traction Motors:** Four EE507 of 185 kW.
**Dimensions:** 19.75 x 2.82 m.
**Maximum Speed:** 90 mph.

**62121 – 40. MBSO.** Dia. ED261. Lot No. 30760 Derby 1967. 58S. 49 t.
**62182 – 216. MBSO.** Dia. ED261. Lot No. 30773 York 1967 – 68. 58S. 49 t.
**62217 – 66. MBSO.** Dia. ED263. Lot No. 30794 York 1968 – 69. 58S. 49 t.
**62267 – 76. MBSO.** Dia. ED263. Lot No. 30800 York 1970. 58S. 49 t.
**62317 – 54. MBSO.** Dia. ED263. Lot No. 30813 York 1970 – 73. 58S. 49 t.
**62435 – 75. MBSO.** Dia. ED263. Lot No. 30851 York 1973 – 74. 58S. 49 t.
**70781 – 800. TSO.** Dia. EH276. Lot No. 30759 Derby 1967. 98S. 31.5 t.
**70872 – 906. TSO.** Dia. EH276. Lot No. 30772 York 1967 – 68. 98S. 31.5 t.
**70907 – 56. TSO.** Dia. EH283. Lot No. 30793 York 1968 – 69. 98S. 31.5 t.
**70957 – 66. TSO.** Dia. EH283. Lot No. 30801 York 1970. 98S. 31.5 t.
**70997 – 71034. TSO.** Dia. EH283. Lot No. 30812 York 1970 – 73. 98S. 31.5 t.
**71115 – 55. TSO.** Dia. EH283. Lot No. 30852 York 1973 – 74. 98S. 31.5 t.
**76230 – 69. DTCsoL.** Dia. EE365. Lot No. 30758 York 1967. 18F 46S 1L. 35 t.
**76333 – 402. DTCsoL.** Dia. EE365. Lot No. 30771 Yk 1967 – 68. 18F 46S 1L. 35 t.
**76441 – 540. DTCsoL.** Dia. EE367. Lot No. 30792 Yk 1968 – 69. 18F 46S 1L. 35 t.
**76541 – 60. DTCsoL.** Dia. EE367. Lot No. 30799 York 1970. 18F 46S 1L. 35 t.
**76641 – 716. DTCsoL.** Dia. EE367. Lot No. 30811 Yk 1970 – 73. 18F 46S 1L. 35 t.
**76861 – 942. DTCsoL.** Dia. EE368. Lot No. 30853 Yk 1973 – 74. 18F 46S 1L. 35 t.

* Fitted with fluorescent lighting and PA.

## 3001 – 3169

Renumbered from 7700 – 7894 respectively with the last three digits unchanged.

| | | | | | | | | |
|------|---|---|------|-----|-------|-------|-------|-------|
| 3001 | * | N | NSBX | WD | 76230 | 62121 | 70781 | 76231 |
| 3002 | | N | NSBX | WD | 76233 | 62122 | 70782 | 76232 |
| 3003 | | N | NSBX | WD | 76234 | 62123 | 70783 | 76235 |
| 3006 | * | N | NSBX | WD | 76241 | 62126 | 70786 | 76240 |
| 3007 | | N | NSBX | WD | 76243 | 62127 | 70787 | 76242 |
| 3008 | * | N | NSBX | WD | 76244 | 62128 | 70788 | 76245 |
| 3009 | * | N | NSBX | WD | 76246 | 62129 | 70789 | 76247 |
| 3010 | * | N | NSBX | WD | 76369 | 62130 | 70790 | 76249 |
| 3012 | * | N | NSBX | WD | 76252 | 62132 | 70792 | 76253 |
| 3013 | * | N | NSBX | WD | 76255 | 62133 | 70793 | 76254 |
| 3014 | * | N | NSBX | WD | 76257 | 62134 | 70794 | 76248 |
| 3015 | | N | NSBX | WD | 76258 | 62135 | 70795 | 76259 |
| 3016 | * | N | NSBX | WD | 76261 | 62339 | 70796 | 76260 |
| 3017 | | N | NSBX | WD | 76262 | 62137 | 70797 | 76263 |
| 3018 | * | N | NSBX | WD | 76265 | 62138 | 70875 | 76264 |
| 3019 | * | N | NSBX | WD | 76267 | 62349 | 70799 | 76266 |
| 3020 | * | N | NSBX | WD | 76269 | 62140 | 70800 | 76268 |
| 3026 | * | N | NSBX | WD | 76344 | 62187 | 70877 | 76343 |
| 3030 | * | N | NSBX | WD | 76352 | 62191 | 70881 | 76351 |
| 3032 | | N | NSBX | WD | 76356 | 62193 | 70883 | 76355 |
| 3034 | | N | NSBX | WD | 76360 | 62195 | 70885 | 76359 |
| 3035 | | N | NSBX | WD | 76362 | 62196 | 70890 | 76361 |
| 3037 | | N | NSBX | WD | 76366 | 62198 | 70888 | 76365 |
| 3046 | | N | NSBX | WD | 76384 | 62207 | 70897 | 76383 |
| 3075 | | N | NSBX | WD | 76480 | 62236 | 70926 | 76479 |
| 3078 | * | N | NSBX | WD | 76486 | 62239 | 70929 | 76485 |
| 3080 | * | N | NSXX | BI | 76490 | 62241 | 70931 | 76489 |
| 3092 | | N | NSXX | BI | 76514 | 62253 | 70943 | 76513 |
| 3093 | | N | NSXX | BI | 76516 | 62254 | 70944 | 76515 |
| 3134 | | N | NSXX | BI | 76677 | 62335 | 71015 | 76678 |
| 3139 | * | N | NSXX | BI | 76687 | 62340 | 71020 | 76688 |
| 3147 | * | N | NSXX | BI | 76703 | 62348 | 71028 | 76704 |
| 3149 | * | N | NSXX | BI | 76707 | 62350 | 71030 | 76708 |
| 3152 | * | N | NSXX | BI | 76465 | 62353 | 71033 | 76714 |
| 3153 | * | N | NSBX | WD | 76715 | 62354 | 71034 | 76716 |
| 3154 | * | N | NSBX | WD | 76861 | 62435 | 71115 | 76862 |
| 3155 | * | N | NSBX (3540) WD (RN) | | 76863 | 62238 | 71116 | 76864 |
| 3156 | * | N | NSBX | WD | 76865 | 62437 | 71117 | 76866 |
| 3157 | * | N | NSBX | WD | 76867 | 62438 | 71118 | 76868 |
| 3158 | * | N | NSBX | WD | 76869 | 62439 | 71119 | 76870 |
| 3159 | | N | NSBX | WD | 76871 | 62440 | 71120 | 76872 |
| 3160 | * | N | NSBX | WD | 76873 | 62441 | 71121 | 76874 |
| 3161 | * | N | NKCX | RE | 76875 | 62442 | 71122 | 76876 |
| 3162 | * | N | NKCX | RE | 76877 | 62443 | 71123 | 76878 |
| 3163 | | N | NKCX | RE | 76879 | 62444 | 71124 | 76880 |
| 3164 | | N | NKCX | RE | 76881 | 62445 | 71125 | 76882 |
| 3165 | * | N | NKCX | RE | 76883 | 62446 | 71126 | 76884 |
| 3166 | * | N | NKCX | RE | 76885 | 62447 | 71127 | 76886 |
| 3167 | * | N | NKCX | RE | 76887 | 62448 | 71128 | 76888 |
| 3169 | | N | NKCX | RE | 76891 | 62450 | 71130 | 76892 |

| | | | | | | | | |
|---|---|---|---|---|---|---|---|---|
| 3170 | * | N | NKCX | RE | 76893 | 62451 | 71131 | 76894 |
| 3171 | * | N | NKCX | RE | 76895 | 62452 | 71132 | 76896 |
| 3172 | * | N | NKCX | RE | 76897 | 62453 | 71133 | 76898 |
| 3173 | * | N | NKCX | RE | 76899 | 62454 | 71134 | 76900 |
| 3175 | * | N | NKCX | RE | 76903 | 62456 | 71136 | 76904 |
| 3176 | * | N | NKCX | RE | 76905 | 62457 | 71137 | 76906 |
| 3177 | * | N | NKCX | RE | 76907 | 62458 | 71138 | 76908 |
| 3178 | * | N | NKCX | RE | 76909 | 62463 | 71139 | 76910 |
| 3179 | * | N | NKCX | RE | 76911 | 62460 | 71140 | 76912 |
| 3180 | * | N | NKCX | RE | 76913 | 62461 | 71141 | 76914 |
| 3181 | | N | NKCX | RE | 76915 | 62462 | 71142 | 76916 |
| 3182 | * | N | NKCX | RE | 76917 | 62463 | 71143 | 76918 |
| 3183 | * | N | NKCX | RE | 76919 | 62464 | 71144 | 76920 |
| 3184 | | N | NKCX | RE | 76921 | 62465 | 71145 | 76922 |
| 3185 | | N | NKCX | RE | 76923 | 62466 | 71146 | 76924 |
| 3186 | | N | NKCX | RE | 76925 | 62467 | 71147 | 76926 |
| 3187 | * | N | NKCX | RE | 76927 | 62468 | 71148 | 76928 |
| 3188 | * | N | NKCX | RE | 76929 | 62469 | 71149 | 76930 |
| 3189 | * | N | NKCX | RE | 76931 | 62470 | 71150 | 76932 |
| 3190 | * | N | NKCX | RE | 76933 | 62471 | 71151 | 76934 |
| 3191 | | N | NKCX | RE | 76935 | 62472 | 71152 | 76936 |
| 3192 | | N | NKCX | RE | 76937 | 62473 | 71153 | 76938 |
| 3193 | | N | NKCX | RE | 76939 | 62474 | 71154 | 76940 |
| 3194 | | N | NKCX | RE | 76941 | 62475 | 71155 | 76942 |

## CLASS 413/2     4 Cap

DTCsoL – MBSO – MLSO – DTSsoL. Formed 1982 by the combination of pairs of class 414 (2 Hap) units. Driving equipment removed from motor cars, plus one set of guard's equipment. Driving trailers all declassified.

**Electrical Equipment:** 1951-type.
**Bogies:** Mk. 4.
**Gangways:** Non-gangwayed.
**Traction Motors:** Two EE507 of 185 kW.
**Dimensions:** 19.49 x 2.82 m.
**Maximum Speed:** 90 mph.

All built at Eastleigh on frames laid at Ashford.

**65393 – 65396. MBSO/MLSO.** Dia. EB269. Lot No. 30314 1957. 84S. 42 t.
**65398 – 65401. MBSO/MLSO.** Dia. EB269. Lot No. 30319 1957. 84S. 42 t.
**65404 – 65429. MBSO/MLSO.** Dia. EB269. Lot No. 30388 1958. 84S. 42 t.
**77115 – 77118. DTCsoL.** Dia. EE221. Lot No. 30316 1957. 19F 50S 2L. 32.5 t.
**77123. DTCsoL.** Dia. EE221. Lot No. 30320 1957. 19F 50S 2L. 32.5 t.
**77126 – 77150. DTCsoL.** Dia. EE221. Lot No. 30389 1958. 19F 50S 2L. 32.5 t.

| | | | | | | | |
|---|---|---|---|---|---|---|---|
| 3201 | N | NKSX | GI | 77120 | 65398 | 65401 | 77123 |
| 3202 | N | NKSX | SG | 77118 | 65396 | 65412 | 77134 |
| 3203 | N | NKSX | SG | 77117 | 65395 | 65424 | 77146 |
| 3204 | N | NKCX | SG | 77132 | 65410 | 65420 | 77142 |
| 3205 | N | NKCX | SG | 77135 | 65413 | 65422 | 77144 |
| 3207 | N | NKCX | SG | 77126 | 65404 | 65428 | 77150 |

| 3208 | N | NKCX | SG | 77147 65425 65429 77537 |
|---|---|---|---|---|
| 3211 | N | NKCX | SG | 77115 65393 65427 77149 |

## CLASS 413/3 4 Cap

DTCsoL – MBSO – MLSO – DTCsoL. Formed 1982 by the combination of pairs of class 414 (2 Hap) units. Driving equipment removed from motor cars, plus one set of guard's equipment. Driving trailers all declassified.

**Electrical Equipment:** 1957-type.
**Bogies:** Mk. 4.
**Gangways:** Non-gangwayed.
**Traction Motors:** Two EE507 of 185 kW.
**Dimensions:** 19.49 x 2.82 m.
**Maximum Speed:** 90 mph.

**MBSO/MLSO.** Dia. EB270. Lot No. 30452 Ashford/Eastleigh 1958 – 59. 84S. 42 t.
**DTCsoL.** Dia. EE222. Lot No. 30453 Ashford/Eastleigh 1958 – 59. 19F 50S 2L. 32.5 t.

| 3301 | N | NKSX | SG | 75373 61253 61255 75375 |
|---|---|---|---|---|
| 3302 | N | NKSX | SG | 75361 61241 61244 75364 |
| 3303 | N | NKSX | SG | 75370 61250 61252 75372 |
| 3304 | N | NKSX | SG | 75402 61282 61283 75403 |
| 3305 | N | NKSX | SG | 75399 61279 61302 75422 |
| 3306 | N | NKSX | SG | 75374 61254 61256 75376 |
| 3307 | N | NKSX | SG | 75378 61258 61271 75391 |
| 3311 | N | NKSX | SG | 75411 61291 61297 75417 |

New batch being formed with the motor cars as outer vehicles. MBSO – 2DTCsoL – MBSO.

| 3321 | N | NKSX | SG | 61268 75388 75398 61278 |
|---|---|---|---|---|
| 3322 | N | NKSX | SG | 61262 75382 75415 61295 |
| 3323 | N | NKSX | SG | 61273 75393 75420 61300 |
| 3324 | N | NKSX | SG | 61270 75390 75423 61303 |
| 3325 | N | NKSX | SG | 61261 75381 75418 61298 |

## CLASS 423/1 Facelifted 4 Vep.

DTCsoL – MBSO – TSO – DTCsoL. For details see 3000 series. Facelifted with fluorescent lighting, PA. The MBSO has been modified to seat 76S.

| 3404 | (3441) | N | NSBX | WD | 76378 62261 70894 76236 |
|---|---|---|---|---|---|
| 3405 | (3005) | N | NSBX | WD | 76239 62271 70785 76238 |
| 3411 | (3011) | N | NSBX | WD | 76251 62342 70791 76250 |
| 3421 | (3168) | N | NKCX | RE | 76889 62449 71129 76890 |
| 3422 | (3040) | N | NKCX | RE | 76372 62201 70891 76371 |
| 3423 | (3061) | N | NKCX | RE | 76452 62222 70912 76451 |
| 3424 | (3031) | N | NKCX | RE | 76354 62185 70882 76353 |
| 3425 | (3023) | N | NSBX | WD | 76338 62192 70874 76358 |
| 3426 | (3047) | N | NSBX | WD | 76386 62208 70898 76385 |
| 3427 | (3041) | N | NSBX | WD | 76374 62184 70892 76373 |
| 3428 | (3062) | N | NSBX | WD | 76454 62223 70913 76453 |

| | | | | | | | | |
|---|---|---|---|---|---|---|---|---|
| 3429 | (3021) | N | NSBX | WD | 76334 | 62202 | 70872 | 76333 |
| 3430 | (3028) | N | NSBX | WD | 76348 | 62189 | 70879 | 76347 |
| 3431 | (3064) | N | NSBX | WD | 76458 | 62182 | 70915 | 76457 |
| 3432 | (3054) | N | NSBX | WD | 76400 | 62225 | 70905 | 76399 |
| 3433 | (3057) | N | NSBX | WD | 76444 | 62215 | 70908 | 76443 |
| 3434 | (3066) | N | NSBX | WD | 76462 | 62218 | 70917 | 76461 |
| 3435 | (3025) | N | NSXX | BI | 76342 | 62228 | 70876 | 76341 |
| 3436 | (3029) | N | NSXX | BI | 76350 | 62190 | 70880 | 76349 |
| 3437 | (3027) | N | NSXX | BI | 76346 | 62186 | 70878 | 76345 |
| 3438 | (3100) | N | NSXX | BI | 76530 | 62262 | 70951 | 76529 |
| 3439 | (3055) | N | NSXX | BI | 76402 | 62227 | 70906 | 76401 |
| 3440 | (3102) | N | NSXX | BI | 76534 | 62188 | 70953 | 76533 |
| 3442 | (3081) | N | NSXX | BI | 76492 | 62216 | 70932 | 76491 |
| 3443 | (3082) | N | NSXX | BI | 76494 | 62263 | 70933 | 76493 |
| 3444 | (3038) | N | NSXX | BI | 76368 | 62204 | 70889 | 76367 |
| 3445 | (3060) | N | NKCX | RE | 76450 | 62242 | 70911 | 76449 |
| 3446 | (3101) | N | NKCX | RE | 76532 | 62243 | 70952 | 76531 |
| 3447 | (3044) | N | NKCX | RE | 76380 | 62199 | 70895 | 76379 |
| 3448 | (3042) | N | NKCX | RE | 76376 | 62221 | 70886 | 76375 |
| 3449 | (3022) | N | NKCX | RE | 76336 | 62205 | 70873 | 76335 |
| 3450 | (3060) | N | NKCX | RE | 76460 | 62203 | 70916 | 76459 |
| 3451 | (3079) | N | NKCX | RE | 76488 | 62240 | 70930 | 76487 |
| 3452 | | N | NKCX | RE | 76340 | 62183 | 71021 | 76690 |
| 3453 | (3045) | N | NKCX | RE | 76382 | 62226 | 70896 | 76381 |
| 3454 | | N | NKCX | RE | 76390 | 62200 | 70798 | 76389 |
| 3455 | (3048) | N | NSBX | WD | 76388 | 62206 | 70899 | 76387 |
| 3456 | (3063) | N | NSBX | WD | 76456 | 62210 | 70914 | 76455 |
| 3457 | (3050) | N | NSBX | WD | 76392 | 62197 | 70901 | 76391 |
| 3458 | (3051) | N | NSBX | WD | 76394 | 62209 | 70902 | 76393 |
| 3459 | (3052) | N | NSBX | WD | 76396 | 62224 | 70903 | 76395 |
| 3460 | (3105) | N | NSXX | BI | 76540 | 62211 | 70956 | 76539 |
| 3461 | (3104) | N | NSXX | BI | 76538 | 62212 | 70955 | 76537 |
| 3462 | (3103) | N | NSXX | BI | 76536 | 62213 | 70954 | 76535 |
| 3463 | (3053) | N | NSXX | BI | 76398 | 62266 | 70904 | 76397 |
| 3464 | (3056) | N | NSXX | BI | 76442 | 62265 | 70907 | 76441 |
| 3465 | (3106) | N | NSXX | BI | 76542 | 62264 | 70957 | 76541 |
| 3466 | (3067) | N | NSBX | WD | 76464 | 62214 | 70918 | 76463 |
| 3467 | (3058) | N | NSBX | WD | 76446 | 62217 | 70909 | 76445 |
| 3468 | (3059) | N | NSBX | WD | 76448 | 62267 | 70910 | 76447 |
| 3469 | (3108) | N | NSBX | WD | 76546 | 62219 | 70959 | 76545 |
| 3470 | (3083) | N | NSBX | WD | 76496 | 62220 | 70934 | 76495 |
| 3471 | (3084) | N | NKCX | RE | 76498 | 62269 | 70935 | 76497 |
| 3472 | (3085) | N | NKCX | RE | 76500 | 62244 | 70936 | 76499 |
| 3473 | (3086) | N | NKCX | RE | 76502 | 62245 | 70937 | 76339 |
| 3474 | (3087) | N | NKCX | RE | 76504 | 62246 | 70938 | 76503 |
| 3475 | (3111) | N | NKCX | RE | 76552 | 62270 | 70962 | 76551 |
| 3476 | (3109) | N | NSXX | BI | 76548 | 62247 | 70960 | 76547 |
| 3477 | (3110) | N | NSXX | BI | 76550 | 62248 | 70961 | 76549 |
| 3478 | (3122) | N | NSXX | BI | 76653 | 62125 | 71003 | 76654 |
| 3479 | (3123) | N | NSBX | WD | 76655 | 62272 | 71004 | 76656 |
| 3480 | (3072) | N | NSBX | WD | 76474 | 62323 | 70923 | 76473 |
| 3481 | (3119) | N | NSBX | WD | 76648 | 62324 | 70900 | 76647 |

| | | | | | | | |
|---|---|---|---|---|---|---|---|
| 3482 | (3124) | N | NSBX | WD | 76657 | 62320 | 71005 | 76658 |
| 3483 | (3126) | N | NSBX | WD | 76661 | 62233 | 71007 | 76662 |
| 3484 | (3073) | N | NSBX | WD | 76476 | 62325 | 70924 | 76475 |
| 3485 | (3089) | N | NSBX | WD | 76508 | 62327 | 70940 | 76507 |
| 3486 | (3074) | N | NSBX | WD | 76478 | 62234 | 70925 | 76477 |
| 3487 | (3090) | N | NSBX | WD | 76510 | 62250 | 70941 | 76509 |
| 3488 | (3127) | N | NSBX | WD | 76663 | 62235 | 71008 | 76664 |
| 3489 | (3128) | N | NSBX | WD | 76665 | 62251 | 71009 | 76666 |
| 3490 | (3143) | N | NSBX | WD | 76695 | 62328 | 71024 | 76696 |
| 3491 | (3076) | N | NKCX | RE | 76337 | 62436 | 70927 | 76481 |
| 3492 | (3129) | N | NKCX | RE | 76667 | 62344 | 71010 | 76668 |
| 3493 | (3130) | N | NKCX | RE | 76669 | 62237 | 71011 | 76670 |
| 3494 | (3133) | N | NKCX | RE | 76675 | 62330 | 71014 | 76676 |
| 3495 | (3145) | N | NKCX | RE | 76699 | 62331 | 71026 | 76700 |
| 3496 | (3132) | N | NKCX | RE | 76673 | 62334 | 71013 | 76674 |
| 3497 | (3131) | N | NKCX | RE | 76671 | 62346 | 71012 | 76672 |
| 3498 | (3146) | N | NKCX | RE | 76701 | 62333 | 71027 | 76702 |
| 3499 | (3174) | N | NKCX | RE | 76901 | 62347 | 71135 | 76902 |
| 3500 | (3070) | N | NKCX | RE | 76470 | 62455 | 70921 | 76469 |
| 3501 | (3091) | N | NSXX | BI | 76512 | 62332 | 70942 | 76511 |
| 3502 | (3150) | N | NSXX | BI | 76709 | 62252 | 71031 | 76710 |
| 3503 | (3136) | N | NSXX | BI | 76681 | 62231 | 71017 | 76682 |
| 3504 | (3151) | N | NSXX | BI | 76711 | 62351 | 71032 | 76712 |
| 3505 | (3071) | N | NSXX | BI | 76472 | 62352 | 70922 | 76471 |
| 3506 | (3112) | N | NSXX | BI | 76554 | 62317 | 70963 | 76553 |
| 3507 | (3114) | N | NSXX | BI | 76558 | 62232 | 70965 | 76557 |
| 3508 | (3117) | N | NSBX | WD | 76643 | 62273 | 70998 | 76644 |
| 3509 | (3115) | N | NSBX | WD | 76560 | 62275 | 70966 | 76559 |
| 3510 | (3116) | N | NSBX | WD | 76641 | 62318 | 70997 | 76642 |
| 3511 | (3118) | N | NSBX | WD | 76645 | 62276 | 70999 | 76646 |
| 3512 | (3135) | N | NSXX | BI | 76679 | 62337 | 71016 | 76680 |
| 3513 | (3141) | N | NSXX | BI | 76691 | 62336 | 71022 | 76692 |
| 3514 | (3137) | N | NSXX | BI | 76683 | 62136 | 71018 | 76684 |
| 3515 | (3107) | N | NSXX | BI | 76544 | 62319 | 70958 | 76543 |
| 3516 | (3142) | N | NSBX | WD | 76693 | 62268 | 71023 | 76694 |
| 3517 | (3138) | N | NSXX | BI | 76685 | 62338 | 71019 | 76686 |
| 3518 | (3140) | N | NSXX | BI | 76689 | 62343 | 70887 | 76363 |
| 3519 | (3113) | N | NSBX | WD | 76556 | 62274 | 70964 | 76555 |
| 3520 | (3144) | N | NSBX | WD | 76697 | 62311 | 71025 | 76698 |
| 3521 | (3077) | N | NSBX | WD | 76484 | 62345 | 70928 | 76483 |
| 3522 | (3148) | N | NSXX | BI | 76705 | 62341 | 71029 | 76706 |
| 3523 | (3121) | N | NSBX | WD | 76651 | 62139 | 71002 | 76652 |
| 3524 | (3068) | N | NSBX | WD | 76466 | 62322 | 70919 | 76370 |
| 3525 | (3096) | N | NSXX | BI | 76522 | 62229 | 70947 | 76521 |
| 3526 | (3097) | N | NSXX | BI | 76524 | 62255 | 70948 | 76523 |
| 3527 | (3095) | N | NSXX | BI | 76520 | 62326 | 70946 | 76519 |
| 3528 | (3094) | N | NSXX | BI | 76518 | 62258 | 70945 | 76517 |
| 3529 | (3125) | N | NSBX | WD | 76659 | 62257 | 71006 | 76660 |
| 3530 | (3069) | N | NSBX | WD | 76468 | 62256 | 70920 | 76467 |
| 3531 | (3120) | N | NSBX | WD | 76649 | 62230 | 71001 | 76650 |
| 3532 | (3099) | N | NSXX | BI | 76528 | 62321 | 70950 | 76527 |
| 3533 | (3098) | N | NSXX | BI | 76364 | 62260 | 70949 | 76525 |

| | | | | | | | |
|---|---|---|---|---|---|---|---|
| 3534 | (3088) | N | NSXX | BI | 76506 | 62259 | 70939 76505 |
| 3535 | ( ) | | | | | | |
| 3536 | ( ) | | | | | | |
| 3537 | ( ) | | | | | | |
| 3538 | ( ) | | | | | | |
| 3539 | ( ) | | | | | | |
| 3540 | (3155) | | | | | | |
| 3541 | ( ) | | | | | | |
| 3542 | ( ) | | | | | | |
| 3543 | ( ) | | | | | | |
| 3544 | ( ) | | | | | | |
| 3545 | ( ) | | | | | | |
| 3546 | ( ) | | | | | | |
| 3547 | ( ) | | | | | | |
| 3548 | ( ) | | | | | | |
| 3549 | ( ) | | | | | | |
| 3550 | ( ) | | | | | | |
| 3551 | ( ) | | | | | | |
| Spare | | | | | 62249 | | |

## CLASS 414/3 — 2 Hap

DMBSO – DTCsoL.

**Electrical Equipment:** 1957-type.
**Bogies:** Mk. 4.
**Gangways:** Non-gangwayed.
**Traction Motors:** Two EE507 of 185 kW.
**Dimensions:** 19.49 x 2.82 m.
**Maximum Speed:** 90 mph.

**DMBSO.** Dia. EB270. Lot No. 30452 Ashford/Eastleigh 1959. 84S. 42 t.
**DTCsoL.** Dia. EE362. Lot No. 30453 Ashford/Eastleigh 1959. 19F 60S 1L. 32.5 t.

| | | | | | |
|---|---|---|---|---|---|
| 4308 | N | NKCX | RE | 61275 | 75395 |
| 4309 | N | NKCX | RE | 61276 | 75396 |
| 4311 | N | NKCX | RE | 61287 | 75407 |
| 4313 | N | NKCX | RE | 61290 | 75410 |
| 4314 | N | NKCX | RE | 61294 | 75414 |

## CLASS 405 — 1936 type 4 Sub

DMBSO – TS – TSO – DMBSO. This unit is kept for special workings and is not compatible electrically with other SR EMUs. It has automatic air brakes, but no electro-pneumatic brakes.

**Electrical Equipment:** 1936-type.
**Bogies:** Central 43'' motor bogies and SR standard trailer bogies.
**Gangways:** Non-gangwayed.
**Traction Motors:** Two EE507 of 185 kW.
**Dimensions:** 19.05 x 2.82 m. (outer cars), 18.90 x 2.82 m (inner cars).
**Maximum Speed:** 75 mph.

**DMBSO**. Dia. EB265. Lot No. 3638 Eastleigh 1951. 82S. 42 t.
**TS**. Dia. EH262. Lot No. 3351 Eastleigh 1947. 120S. 27 t.
**TSO**. Dia. EH266. Lot No. 3384 Eastleigh 1948. 102S. 26 t.

| 4732 | **SG** NSXX | BI | 12795 10239 12354 12796 |
|---|---|---|---|

# CLASS 415/1        SR DESIGN 4 EPB

DMBSO – 2TSO – DMBSO. Originally formed with a TS and a TSO, but all except 5001 now have 2TSO.

**Electrical Equipment:** 1951-type.
**Bogies:** Central 40'' motor bogies and SR standard trailer bogies.
**Gangways:** Non-gangwayed.
**Traction Motors:** Two EE507 of 185 kW.
**Dimensions:** 19.05 x 2.82 m. (outer cars), 18.90 x 2.82 m (inner cars).
**Maximum Speed:** 75 mph (90 mph e).
**Non-standard livery:** Southern Region green.

Built to various SR lots as shown, all at Lancing/Eastleigh.

★ Converted from class 405 (4 Sub) TS.

**14001 – 14026. DMBSO.** Dia. EB266. Lot No. 3638 1952. 82S. 40 t.
**14039 – 14053. DMBSO.** Dia. EB266. Lot No. 3756 1953. 82S. 40 t.
**14069 – 14208. DMBSO.** Dia. EB266. Lot No. 3757 1953 – 4. 82S. 40 t.
**14221 – 14310. DMBSO.** Dia. EB266. Lot No. 4016 1954 – 5. 82S. 40 t.
**14311 – 14405. DMBSO.** Dia. EB266. Lot No. 4099 1955 – 6. 82S. 40 t.
**14413 – 14426. DMBSO.** Dia. EB266. Lot No. 4172 1956. 82S. 40 t.
**14433 – 14510. DMBSO.** Dia. EB266. Lot No. 4173 1956 – 7. 82S. 40 t.
**14522 – 14523. DMBSO.** Dia. EB267. Lot No. 4281 1957. 84S. 40 t. Former class 418/0 vehicles.

**15015. TSO★.** Lot No. 3463 1948. 102S. 27 t.
**15101 – 15113. TSO.** Dia. EH270. Lot No. 3638 1951 – 2. 102S. 27 t.
**15118 – 15127. TSO.** Dia. EH270. Lot No. 3756 1953. 102S. 27 t.
**15135 – 15158. TSO.** Dia. EH270. Lot No. 3757 1953 – 4. 102S. 27 t.
**15207. TS.** Dia. EH268. Lot No. 4016 1954 – 55. 120S. 28 t.
**15234 – 15277/279 – 283. TSO.** Dia. EH270. Lot No. 4016 1954 – 5. 102S. 27 t.
**15334 – 15382. TSO.** Dia. EH270. Lot No. 4099 1955 – 6. 102S. 27 t.
**15395 – 15401. TSO.** Dia. EH270. Lot No. 4172 1956. 102S. 27 t.
**15405 – 15444. TSO.** Dia. EH270. Lot No. 4173 1956 – 7. 102S. 27 t.
**65300 – 65310. DMBSO.** Dia. EB269. Lot No. 30114 Ashford/Eastleigh 1954. 84S. 42 t. BR design DMBSOs (ex class 416/2).

| 5001 | **SG** NKSX | SG | 14001 15207 15101 14002 |
|---|---|---|---|
| 5124 | NKSX | SG | 14248 15248 15252 14247 |
| 5131 | NKSX | SG | 14261 15412 15259 14262 |
| 5138 | NKSX | SG | 14275 15423 15266 14276 |
| 5145 | NKSX | SG | 14290 15158 15273 14289 |
| 5153 | NKSX | SG | 14305 15256 15281 14306 |
| 5154 | NKSX | SG | 14308 15279 15282 14307 |
| 5157 | NKSX | SG | 14313 15381 15335 14314 |
| 5159 | NKSX | SG | 14317 15105 15337 14318 |
| 5160 | NKSX | SG | 14319 15268 15338 14320 |

| 5176 | | NKSX | SG | 14352 15396 15354 14351 |
|------|--|------|----|--------------------------|
| 5177 | | NKSX | SG | 14354 15257 15355 14353 |
| 5185 | | NKSX | SG | 14369 15277 15363 14370 |
| 5190 | | NKSX | SG | 14380 15361 15368 14379 |
| 5194 | | NKSX | SG | 14388 15275 15372 14387 |
| 5195 | | NKSX | SG | 14389 15239 15373 14390 |
| 5196 | | NKSX | SG | 14392 15399 15374 14391 |
| 5209 | | NKSX | SG | 14418 15395 15397 14417 |
| 5213 | | NKSX | SG | 14425 15353 15401 14426 |
| 5217 | | NKSX | SG | 14434 15366 15405 14433 |
| 5220 | | NKSX | SG | 14439 15349 15408 14260 |
| 5232 | | NKSX | SG | 14464 15422 15420 14463 |
| 5240 | | NKSX | SG | 14103 15425 15428 14480 |
| 5243 | | NKSX | SG | 14405 15375 15356 14485 |
| 5248 | | NKSX | SG | 14492 15443 15436 14510 |
| 5261 | | NKSX | SG | 65300 15154 15413 65310 |
| 5266 | (5020) | NKSX | SG | 14039 15234 15382 14040 |
| 5268 | (5035) | NKSX | SG | 14069 15113 15135 14070 |
| 5269 | (5039) | NKSX | SG | 14078 15118 15139 14094 |
| 5270 | (5040) | NKSX | SG | 14080 15122 15140 14079 |
| 5275 | (5049) | NKSX | SG | 14098 15271 15149 14097 |
| 5277 | (5052) | NKSX | SG | 14104 15103 15152 14495 |
| 5279 | | NKSX | SG | 14257 15429 15380 14258 |
| 5280 | | NKSX | SG | 14232 15421 15410 14231 |

## CLASS 415/4     FACELIFTED SR DESIGN 4 EPB

DMBSO – 2TSO – DMBSO. Facelifted with new trim, fluorescent lighting, PA.

**Electrical Equipment:** 1951-type.
**Bogies:** Central 40″ motor bogies and SR standard trailer bogies.
**Gangways:** Non-gangwayed.
**Traction Motors:** Two EE507 of 185 kW.
**Dimensions:** 19.05 x 2.82 m. (outer cars), 18.90 x 2.82 m (inner cars).
**Maximum Speed:** 75 mph. (90 mph e).

Built to various SR lots as shown, all at Lancing/Eastleigh.
★ Converted from class 405 (4 Sub) TS. Vehicles in the 154xx series were converted on facelifting.
§ Converted from class 415 TS.

**14003 – 14030. DMBSO.** Dia. EB277. Lot No. 3638 1952. 82S. 40 t.
**14037 – 14066. DMBSO.** Dia. EB277. Lot No. 3756 1953. 82S. 40 t.
**14071 – 14206. DMBSO.** Dia. EB277. Lot No. 3757 1953 – 4. 82S. 40 t.
**14211 – 14304. DMBSO.** Dia. EB277. Lot No. 4016 1954 – 5. 82S. 40 t.
**14315 – 14410. DMBSO.** Dia. EB277. Lot No. 4099 1955 – 6. 82S. 40 t.
**14411 – 14430. DMBSO.** Dia. EB277. Lot No. 4172 1956. 82S. 40 t.
**14431 – 14520. DMBSO.** Dia. EB277. Lot No. 4173 1956 – 7. 82S. 40 t.
**14521 – 14570. DMBSO.** Dia. EB278. Lot No. 4281 1957. 82S. 40 t. Former class 418/0 vehicle or 416/3 vehicles.

**15001/10. 15466/67/71/74/75. TSO★.** Dia. EH270. Lot No. 1094 1946. 102S. 27 t.
**15002/19/23/27/30/39 – 42/48/50. 15450. TSO★.** Lot No. 3351 1947. 102S. 27 t.

15011/20/29/37/44/51/52/56 – 58/61 – 62/65/66/68 – 71/73/75 – 78. TSO★.
Lot No. 3463 1948. 102S. 27 t.
15012/54/74. TSO★. Lot No. 3386 1948. 102S. 27 t.
15033/34/36/45 – 47/53/55/59/60/67. TSO★. Lot No. 3231 1947. 102S. 27 t.
15104 – 15115. TSO. Lot No. 3638 1951 – 2. 102S. 27 t.
15119 – 15128. TSO. Lot No. 3756 1953. 102S. 27 t.
15136 – 15182. TSO§. Lot No. 3757 1953 – 4. 102S. 27 t.
15184 – 15227/230 – 265. TSO§. Lot No. 4016 1954 – 5. 102S. 27 t.
15285 – 15383. TSO§. Lot No. 4099 1955 – 6. 102S. 27 t.
15384 – 15403. TSO§. Lot No. 4172 1956. 102S. 27 t.
15404 – 15448. TSO. Lot No. 4173 1956 – 7. 102S. 27 t.
15449/65/79/80. TSO★. Lot No. 3384 1948. 102S. 27 t.
15451. TSO★. Lot No. 3617 1948. 102S. 27 t.
15452/59/61/64/69/73. TSO★. Lot No. 3504 1949. 102S. 27 t.
15453/63. TSO★. Lot No. 3385 1948. 102S. 27 t.
15454/56/57/58/60/62/68/70/72/76/78. TSO★. Lot No. 3464 1949. 102S.
27 t.
15481. TSO★. Lot No. 3505 1950. 102S. 27 t.
15455/77. TSO★. Lot No. 3506 1950. 102S. 27 t.

e – Express gear ratio.                     * 14211 is blue and grey.

| | | | | | | | |
|---|---|---|---|---|---|---|---|
| 5401 | e | **N** | NKSX | SG | 14556 | 15449 | 15450 | 14521 |
| 5402 | | | NKSX | SG | 14449 | 15020 | 15351 | 14407 |
| 5403 | | **N** | NSLX | SU | 14286 | 15174 | 15221 | 14285 |
| 5404 | | | NKSX | SG | 14435 | 15036 | 15406 | 14436 |
| 5405 | | **N** | NKSX | SG | 14470 | 15053 | 15216 | 14469 |
| 5407 | | **N** | NKSX | SG | 14396 | 15392 | 15060 | 14427 |
| 5408 | | | NKSX | SG | 14297 | 15227 | 15313 | 14298 |
| 5409 | | **N** | NKSX | SG | 14494 | 15065 | 15047 | 14206 |
| 5410 | e | **N** | NKSX | SG | 14527 | 15386 | 15304 | 14528 |
| 5411 | | **N** | NKSX | SG | 14475 | 15056 | 15192 | 14476 |
| 5412 | | | NKSX | SG | 14415 | 15451 | 15452 | 14304 |
| 5413 | | **N** | NKSX | SG | 14428 | 15326 | 15191 | 14395 |
| 5414 | | **N** | NSLX | SU | 14441 | 15039 | 15182 | 14442 |
| 5415 | | **N** | NSLX | SU | 14465 | 15040 | 15051 | 14466 |
| 5419 | | **N** | NKSX | SG | 14473 | 15055 | 15058 | 14474 |
| 5421 | | **N** | NSLX | SU | 14500 | 15068 | 15073 | 14499 |
| 5422 | | **N** | NKSX | SG | 14467 | 15209 | 15050 | 14468 |
| 5423 | | **N** | NKSX | SG | 14511 | 15074 | 15212 | 14512 |
| 5424 | | **N** | NKSX | SG | 14447 | 15042 | 15052 | 14448 |
| 5425 | e | **N** | NSLX | SU | 14538 | 15453 | 15454 | 14570 |
| 5426 | | **N** | NKSX | SG | 14517 | 15077 | 15066 | 14518 |
| 5427 | | **N** | NKSX | SG | 14453 | 15045 | 15046 | 14454 |
| 5428 | | **N** | NKSX | SG | 14430 | 15393 | 15061 | 14429 |
| 5429 | | **N** | NKSX | SG | 14410 | 15333 | 15383 | 14409 |
| 5430 | | **N** | NKSX | SG | 14496 | 15438 | 15437 | 14509 |
| 5431 | | **N** | NKSX | SG | 14423 | 15390 | 15400 | 14424 |
| 5432 | | **N** | NKSX | SG | 14486 | 15044 | 15447 | 14416 |
| 5433 | | **N** | NKSX | SG | 14472 | 15054 | 15424 | 14471 |
| 5434 | | **N** | NKSX | SG | 14498 | 15067 | 15455 | 14497 |
| 5435 | | **N** | NKSX | SG | 14491 | 15403 | 15431 | 14267 |
| 5436 | | **N** | NKSX | SG | 14534 | 15456 | 15457 | 14543 |

| | | | | | | | |
|---|---|---|---|---|---|---|---|
| 5437 | N | NKSX | SG | 14411 | 15384 | 15394 | 14412 |
| 5438 | N | NKSX | SG | 14530 | 15459 | 15458 | 14547 |
| 5441 | N | NKSX | SG | 14397 | 15327 | 15377 | 14398 |
| 5442 | N | NKSX | SG | 14537 | 15460 | 15461 | 14554 |
| 5443 | N | NKSX | SG | 14504 | 15070 | 15440 | 14503 |
| 5444 | N | NKSX | SG | 14535 | 15463 | 15462 | 14553 |
| 5445 | N | NKSX | SG | 14540 | 15464 | 15465 | 14529 |
| 5446 | N | NKSX | SG | 14531 | 15466 | 15467 | 14541 |
| 5447 | N | NKSX | SG | 14532 | 15468 | 15469 | 14550 |
| 5448 | N | NKSX | SG | 14539 | 15470 | 15471 | 14548 |
| 5449 | | NKSX | SG | 14438 | 15291 | 15407 | 14437 |
| 5452 | e N | NKSX | SG | 14536 | 15477 | 15476 | 14563 |
| 5453 | e | NKSX | SG | 14545 | 15479 | 15478 | 14525 |
| 5454 | e N | NKSX | SG | 14555 | 15481 | 15480 | 14524 |
| 5455 | N | NKSX | SG | 14062 | 15023 | 15027 | 14054 |
| 5456 | N | NKSX | SG | 14482 | 15059 | 15001 | 14481 |
| 5457 | N | NKSX | SG | 14502 | 15069 | 15439 | 14501 |
| 5458 | N | NKSX | SG | 14431 | 15034 | 15404 | 14432 |
| 5459 | N | NKSX | SG | 14505 | 15071 | 15441 | 14506 |
| 5460 | N | NKSX | SG | 14515 | 15076 | 15446 | 14516 |
| 5461 | N | NKSX | SG | 14519 | 15078 | 15448 | 14520 |
| 5462 | N | NKSX | SG | 14021 | 15011 | 15111 | 14022 |
| 5463 | N | NKSX | SG | 14037 | 15019 | 15119 | 14038 |
| 5464 | N | NKSX | SG | 14081 | 15166 | 15159 | 14082 |
| 5465 | | NKSX | SG | 14236 | 15196 | 15208 | 14350 |
| 5466 | | NKSX | SG | 14004 | 15002 | 15220 | 14003 |
| 5467 | N | NKSX | SG | 14006 | 15062 | 15177 | 14005 |
| 5470 | | NKSX | SG | 14315 | 15286 | 15215 | 14316 |
| 5471 | N | NKSX | SG | 14255 | 15206 | 15231 | 14256 |
| 5472 | | NKSX | SG | 14508 | 15295 | 15169 | 14458 |
| 5473 | | NKSX | SG | 14493 | 15029 | 15170 | 14058 |
| 5474 | | NKSX | SG | 14065 | 15033 | 15224 | 14066 |
| 5475 | | NKSX | SG | 14019 | 15010 | 15048 | 14020 |
| 5477 | | NKSX | SG | 14013 | 15180 | 15233 | 14057 |
| 5478 | | NKSX | SG | 14059 | 15030 | 15167 | 14060 |
| 5479 | | NKSX | SG | 14322 | 15289 | 15317 | 14321 |
| 5481 | | NKSX | SG | 14330 | 15293 | 15226 | 14329 |
| 5482 | | NKSX | SG | 14017 | 15009 | 15297 | 14018 |
| 5483 | | NKSX | SG | 14052 | 15175 | 15329 | 14051 |
| 5485 | N | NKSX | SG | 14105 | 15178 | 15185 | 14106 |
| 5486 | N* | NKSX | SG | 14211 | 15161 | 15125 | 14072 |
| 5487 | N | NKSX | SG | 14361 | 15309 | 15359 | 14362 |
| 5488 | N | NKSX | SG | 14386 | 15321 | 15371 | 14385 |
| 5489 | N | NKSX | SG | 14024 | 15012 | 15112 | 14023 |
| 5490 | N | NKSX | SG | 14056 | 15433 | 15128 | 14205 |
| 5491 | N | NKSX | SG | 14029 | 15136 | 15115 | 14030 |
| 5492 | N | NKSX | SG | 14223 | 15246 | 15240 | 14224 |
| 5493 | N | NKSX | SG | 14028 | 15237 | 15114 | 14027 |
| 5494 | N | NKSX | SG | 14073 | 15236 | 15137 | 14074 |
| 5495 | N | NKSX | SG | 14095 | 15265 | 15148 | 14096 |
| 5496 | N | NKSX | SG | 14400 | 15336 | 15378 | 14399 |
| 5497 | N | NKSX | SG | 14246 | 15104 | 15251 | 14245 |

Old numbers of cars converted from class 405:

| | 0 | 1 | 2 | 3 | 4 | 5 | 6 | 7 | 8 | 9 |
|---|---|---|---|---|---|---|---|---|---|---|
| 15000 – 9 | | 10398 | 10345 | 10333 | 10203 | 11454 | 10253 | 10228 | 10335 | 10201 |
| 15010 – 9 | 10391 | 10174 | 10169 | 10189 | 10184 | 10277 | 10251 | 10292 | 10238 | 10332 |
| 15020 – 9 | 10177 | 10254 | 10175 | 10309 | 10266 | 10456 | 10298 | 10281 | 10272 | 10202 |
| 15030 – 9 | 10278 | 10192 | 10280 | 10460 | 10470 | 10229 | 10459 | 10222 | 11451 | 10246 |
| 15040 – 9 | 10285 | 10322 | 10283 | 10275 | 10224 | 10452 | 10466 | 10468 | 10299 | 10176 |
| 15050 – 9 | 10260 | 10211 | 10223 | 10471 | 10167 | 10451 | 10190 | 10193 | 10188 | 10450 |
| 15060 – 9 | 10467 | 10226 | 10178 | 10194 | 10469 | 10212 | 10186 | 10453 | 10183 | 10225 |
| 15070 – 9 | 10180 | 10191 | 10179 | 10185 | 10168 | 10187 | 10227 | 10204 | 10182 | 10195 |
| 15080 – 4 | 11456 | 10208 | 10207 | 10395 | 11485 | | | | | |
| 15450 – 9 | 10337 | 8980 | 12361 | 12360 | 10139 | 12404 | 10133 | 10143 | 10132 | 12381 |
| 15460 – 9 | 10125 | 12393 | 10131 | 12359 | 12389 | 12355 | 10444 | 10448 | 10128 | 12390 |
| 15470 – 9 | 10124 | 10439 | 12391 | 10137 | 10446 | 10445 | 10129 | 12402 | 10141 | 12353 |
| 15480 – 1 | 12358 | 12398 | | | | | | | | |
| | | | | | | | | | | |
| 15449: | 10480 | | | | | | | | | |

# CLASSES 415/6 & 415/7     BR DESIGN 4 EPB

DMBSO(A) – 2TSO – DMBSO(B). All remaining units have been facelifted with new trim, fluorescent lighting and PA. Units with express gear ratio (e) are classified Class 415/7.

**Electrical Equipment:** 1951-type.
**Bogies:** Mark 3C (Mk 3D*) bogies. ★ Mk 3C motor bogie and Mk 3D trailer bogies.
**Gangways:** Non-gangwayed.
**Traction Motors:** Two EE507 of 185 kW.
**Dimensions:** 19.50 x 2.82 m. (outer cars), 19.35 x 2.82 m (inner cars).
**Maximum Speed:** 75 mph (90 mph e).

**DMBSO(A).** Dia. EB271. Lot No. 30582 Eastleigh 1959 – 61. 82S. 41 t.
**DMBSO(B).** Dia. EB272. Lot No. 30582 Eastleigh 1959 – 61. 82S. 41 t.
**TSO.** Dia. EH271. Lot No. 30583 Eastleigh 1959 – 61. 102S. 29.5 t.

e Express gear ratio.

| | | | | | | | |
|---|---|---|---|---|---|---|---|
| 5601 | * | N | NKSX | SG | 61550 | 70409 70410 | 61551 |
| 5602 | | N | NKSX | SG | 61582 | 70441 70442 | 61583 |
| 5603 | * | N | NKSX | SG | 61538 | 70397 70398 | 61539 |
| 5604 | | N | NKSX | SG | 61588 | 70447 70448 | 61589 |
| 5605 | * | N | NKSX | SG | 61540 | 70399 70400 | 61541 |
| 5606 | * | N | NKSX | SG | 61536 | 70395 70396 | 61537 |
| 5610 | | N | NKSX | SG | 61566 | 70425 70426 | 61567 |
| 5611 | | N | NKSX | SG | 61570 | 70429 70430 | 61571 |
| 5612 | * | N | NKSX | SG | 61542 | 70401 70402 | 61543 |
| 5613 | * | N | NKSX | SG | 61532 | 70391 70392 | 61533 |
| 5614 | * | N | NKSX | SG | 61546 | 70405 70406 | 61547 |
| 5615 | | N | NKSX | SG | 61612 | 70471 70472 | 61613 |
| 5616 | | N | NKSX | SG | 61576 | 70435 70436 | 61577 |
| 5617 | | N | NKSX | SG | 61592 | 70451 70452 | 61593 |
| 5619 | | N | NKSX | SG | 61562 | 70421 70422 | 61563 |
| 5620 | | N | NKSX | SG | 61602 | 70461 70462 | 61603 |

| 5621 | * | N | NKSX | SG | 61520 | 70380 | 70379 | 61521 |
| 5622 | | N | NKSX | SG | 61560 | 70419 | 70420 | 61561 |
| 5623 | e | N | NKCX | RE | 61578 | 70437 | 70438 | |
| 5624 | e | N | NKCX | RE | 61572 | 70431 | 70432 | 61573 |
| 5625 | e | N | NKCX | RE | 61608 | 70455 | 70468 | 61609 |
| 5626 | e | N | NKCX | RE | 61590 | 70449 | 70450 | 61591 |
| 5627 | e | N | NKCX | RE | 61600 | 70460 | 70459 | 61601 |
| 5628 | e | N | NKCX | RE | 61604 | 70464 | 70463 | 61605 |

# CLASS 455/7

DTSO – MSO – TSO – DTSO. Sliding doors. Disc brakes. Fluorescent lighting.
PA. Second series with TSOs originally in class 508. Pressure ventilation.

**Bogies:** BT13 (DTSO), BP27 (MSO), BX1 (TSO).
**Gangways:** Through gangwayed.
**Traction Motors:** Four EE507 of 185 kW.
**Dimensions:** 19.83 x 2.82 m. (outer cars), 19.92 x 2.82 m (inner cars).
**Maximum Speed:** 75 mph.

**DTSO.** Dia. EE218. Lot No. 30976 York 1984 – 85. 74S. 29.5 t.
**MSO.** Dia. EC203. Lot No. 30975 York 1984 – 85. 84S. 45 t.
**TSO.** Dia. EH219. Lot No. 30944 York 1977 – 80. 86S. 25.48 t.

| 5701 | N | NSBX | WD | | 77727 | 62783 | 71545 | 77728 |
| 5702 | N | NSBX | WD | | 77729 | 62784 | 71547 | 77730 |
| 5703 | N | NSBX | WD | | 77731 | 62785 | 71540 | 77732 |
| 5704 | N | NSBX | WD | | 77733 | 62786 | 71548 | 77734 |
| 5705 | N | NSBX | WD | | 77735 | 62787 | 71565 | 77736 |
| 5706 | N | NSBX | WD | | 77737 | 62788 | 71534 | 77738 |
| 5707 | N | NSBX | WD | | 77739 | 62789 | 71536 | 77740 |
| 5708 | N | NSBX | WD | | 77741 | 62790 | 71560 | 77742 |
| 5709 | N | NSBX | WD | | 77743 | 62791 | 71532 | 77744 |
| 5710 | N | NSBX | WD | | 77745 | 62792 | 71566 | 77746 |
| 5711 | N | NSBX | WD | | 77747 | 62793 | 71542 | 77748 |
| 5712 | N | NSBX | WD | | 77749 | 62794 | 71546 | 77750 |
| 5713 | N | NSBX | WD | | 77751 | 62795 | 71567 | 77752 |
| 5714 | N | NSBX | WD | | 77753 | 62796 | 71539 | 77754 |
| 5715 | N | NSBX | WD | | 77755 | 62797 | 71535 | 77756 |
| 5716 | N | NSBX | WD | | 77757 | 62798 | 71564 | 77758 |
| 5717 | N | NSBX | WD | | 77759 | 62799 | 71528 | 77760 |
| 5718 | N | NSBX | WD | | 77761 | 62800 | 71557 | 77762 |
| 5719 | N | NSBX | WD | | 77763 | 62801 | 71558 | 77764 |
| 5720 | N | NSBX | WD | | 77765 | 62802 | 71568 | 77766 |
| 5721 | N | NSBX | WD | | 77767 | 62803 | 71553 | 77768 |
| 5722 | N | NSBX | WD | | 77769 | 62804 | 71533 | 77770 |
| 5723 | N | NSBX | WD | | 77771 | 62805 | 71526 | 77772 |
| 5724 | N | NSBX | WD | | 77773 | 62806 | 71561 | 77774 |
| 5725 | N | NSBX | WD | | 77775 | 62807 | 71541 | 77776 |
| 5726 | N | NSBX | WD | | 77777 | 62808 | 71556 | 77778 |
| 5727 | N | NSBX | WD | | 77779 | 62809 | 71562 | 77780 |
| 5728 | N | NSBX | WD | (S) | 77781 | 62810 | 71527 | 77782 |
| 5729 | N | NSBX | WD | | 77783 | 62811 | 71550 | 77784 |

| 5730 | N | NSBX | WD | 77785 62812 71551 77786 |
|------|---|------|-----|-------------------------|
| 5731 | N | NSBX | WD | 77787 62813 71555 77788 |
| 5732 | N | NSBX | WD | 77789 62814 71552 77790 |
| 5733 | N | NSBX | WD | 77791 62815 71549 77792 |
| 5734 | N | NSBX | WD | 77793 62816 71531 77794 |
| 5735 | N | NSBX | WD | 77795 62817 71563 77796 |
| 5736 | N | NSBX | WD | 77797 62818 71554 77798 |
| 5737 | N | NSBX | WD | 77799 62819 71544 77800 |
| 5738 | N | NSBX | WD | 77801 62820 71529 77802 |
| 5739 | N | NSBX | WD | 77803 62821 71537 77804 |
| 5740 | N | NSBX | WD | 77805 62822 71530 77806 |
| 5741 | N | NSBX | WD | 77807 62823 71559 77808 |
| 5742 | N | NSBX | WD | 77809 62824 71543 77810 |
| 5750 | N | NSBX | WD | 77811 62825 71538 77812 |

# CLASS 455/8

DTSO – MSO – TSO – DTSO. Sliding doors. Disc brakes. Fluorescent lighting. PA. First series. Pressure ventilation.

**Bogies:** BP20 (MSO), BT13 (trailer cars).
**Gangways:** Through gangwayed.
**Traction Motors:** Four EE507 of 185 kW.
**Dimensions:** 19.83 x 2.82 m. (outer cars), 19.92 x 2.82 m (inner cars).
**Maximum Speed:** 75 mph.

**DTSO.** Dia. EE218. Lot No. 30972 York 1982 – 84. 74S. 29.5 t.
**MSO.** Dia. EC203. Lot No. 30973 York 1982 – 84. 84S. 45.6 t.
**TSO.** Dia. EH221. Lot No. 30974 York 1982 – 84. 84S. 27.1 t.

| 5801 | N | NSLX | SU | 77579 62709 71637 77580 |
|------|---|------|-----|-------------------------|
| 5802 | N | NSLX | SU | 77581 62710 71664 77582 |
| 5803 | N | NSLX | SU | 77583 62711 71639 77584 |
| 5804 | N | NSLX | SU | 77585 62712 71640 77586 |
| 5805 | N | NSLX | SU | 77587 62713 71641 77588 |
| 5806 | N | NSLX | SU | 77589 62714 71642 77590 |
| 5807 | N | NSLX | SU | 77591 62715 71643 77592 |
| 5808 | N | NSLX | SU | 77593 62716 71644 77594 |
| 5809 | N | NSLX | SU | 77595 62717 71645 77596 |
| 5810 | N | NSLX | SU | 77597 62718 71646 77598 |
| 5811 | N | NSLX | SU | 77599 62719 71647 77600 |
| 5812 | N | NSLX | SU | 77601 62720 71648 77602 |
| 5813 | N | NSLX | SU | 77603 62721 71649 77604 |
| 5814 | N | NSLX | SU | 77605 62722 71650 77606 |
| 5815 | N | NSLX | SU | 77607 62723 71651 77608 |
| 5816 | N | NSLX | SU | 77609 62724 71652 77633 |
| 5817 | N | NSLX | SU | 77611 62725 71653 77612 |
| 5818 | N | NSLX | SU | 77613 62726 71654 77614 |
| 5819 | N | NSLX | SU | 77615 62727 71655 77616 |
| 5820 | N | NSLX | SU | 77617 62728 71656 77618 |
| 5821 | N | NSLX | SU | 77619 62729 71657 77620 |
| 5822 | N | NSLX | SU | 77621 62730 71658 77622 |

| | | | | | | | |
|---|---|---|---|---|---|---|---|
| 5823 | N | NSLX | SU | 77623 | 62731 | 71659 | 77624 |
| 5824 | N | NSLX | SU | 77637 | 62732 | 71660 | 77626 |
| 5825 | N | NSLX | SU | 77627 | 62733 | 71661 | 77628 |
| 5826 | N | NSLX | SU | 77629 | 62734 | 71662 | 77630 |
| 5827 | N | NSLX | SU | 77610 | 62735 | 71663 | 77632 |
| 5828 | N | NSLX | SU | 77634 | 62736 | 71638 | 77631 |
| 5829 | N | NSLX | SU | 77635 | 62737 | 71665 | 77636 |
| 5830 | N | NSLX | SU | 77625 | 62743 | 71666 | 77638 |
| 5831 | N | NSLX | SU | 77639 | 62739 | 71667 | 77640 |
| 5832 | N | NSLX | SU | 77641 | 62740 | 71668 | 77642 |
| 5833 | N | NSLX | SU | 77643 | 62741 | 71669 | 77644 |
| 5834 | N | NSLX | SU | 77645 | 62742 | 71670 | 77646 |
| 5835 | N | NSLX | SU | 77647 | 62738 | 71671 | 77648 |
| 5836 | N | NSLX | SU | 77649 | 62744 | 71672 | 77650 |
| 5837 | N | NSLX | SU | 77651 | 62745 | 71673 | 77652 |
| 5838 | N | NSLX | SU | 77653 | 62746 | 71674 | 77654 |
| 5839 | N | NSLX | SU | 77655 | 62747 | 71675 | 77656 |
| 5840 | N | NSLX | SU | 77657 | 62748 | 71676 | 77658 |
| 5841 | N | NSLX | SU | 77659 | 62749 | 71677 | 77660 |
| 5842 | N | NSLX | SU | 77661 | 62750 | 71678 | 77662 |
| 5843 | N | NSLX | SU | 77663 | 62751 | 71679 | 77664 |
| 5844 | N | NSBX | WD | 77665 | 62752 | 71680 | 77666 |
| 5845 | N | NSBX | WD | 77667 | 62753 | 71681 | 77668 |
| 5846 | N | NSBX | WD | 77669 | 62754 | 71682 | 77670 |
| 5847 | N | NSBX | WD | 77671 | 62755 | 71683 | 77672 |
| 5848 | N | NSBX | WD | 77673 | 62756 | 71684 | 77674 |
| 5849 | N | NSBX | WD | 77675 | 62757 | 71685 | 77676 |
| 5850 | N | NSBX | WD | 77677 | 62758 | 71686 | 77678 |
| 5851 | N | NSBX | WD | 77679 | 62759 | 71687 | 77680 |
| 5852 | N | NSBX | WD | 77681 | 62760 | 71688 | 77682 |
| 5853 | N | NSBX | WD | 77683 | 62761 | 71689 | 77684 |
| 5854 | N | NSBX | WD | 77685 | 62762 | 71690 | 77686 |
| 5855 | N | NSBX | WD | 77687 | 62763 | 71691 | 77688 |
| 5856 | N | NSBX | WD | 77689 | 62764 | 71692 | 77690 |
| 5857 | N | NSBX | WD | 77691 | 62765 | 71693 | 77692 |
| 5858 | N | NSBX | WD | 77693 | 62766 | 71694 | 77694 |
| 5859 | N | NSBX | WD | 77695 | 62767 | 71695 | 77696 |
| 5860 | N | NSBX | WD | 77697 | 62768 | 71696 | 77698 |
| 5861 | N | NSBX | WD | 77699 | 62769 | 71697 | 77700 |
| 5862 | N | NSBX | WD | 77701 | 62770 | 71698 | 77702 |
| 5863 | N | NSBX | WD | 77703 | 62771 | 71699 | 77704 |
| 5864 | N | NSBX | WD | 77705 | 62772 | 71700 | 77706 |
| 5865 | N | NSBX | WD | 77707 | 62773 | 71701 | 77708 |
| 5866 | N | NSBX | WD | 77709 | 62774 | 71702 | 77710 |
| 5867 | N | NSBX | WD | 77711 | 62775 | 71703 | 77712 |
| 5868 | N | NSBX | WD | 77713 | 62776 | 71704 | 77714 |
| 5869 | N | NSBX | WD | 77715 | 62777 | 71705 | 77716 |
| 5870 | N | NSBX | WD | 77717 | 62778 | 71706 | 77718 |
| 5871 | N | NSBX | WD | 77719 | 62779 | 71707 | 77720 |
| 5872 | N | NSBX | WD | 77721 | 62780 | 71708 | 77722 |
| 5873 | N | NSBX | WD | 77723 | 62781 | 71709 | 77724 |
| 5874 | N | NSBX | WD | 77725 | 62782 | 71710 | 77726 |

# CLASS 455/9

DTSO – MSO – TSO – DTSO. Sliding doors. Disc brakes. Fluorescent lighting.
PA. Third series. Convection heating.

**Bogies:** BP20 (MSO), BT13 (trailer cars).
**Gangways:** Through gangwayed.
**Traction Motors:** Four EE507 of 185 kW.
**Dimensions:** 19.83 x 2.82 m. (outer cars), 19.92 x 2.82 m (inner cars).
**Maximum Speed:** 75 mph.

**DTSO.** Dia. EE226. Lot No. 30991 York 1985. 74S. 29.5 t.
**MSO.** Dia. EC206. Lot No. 30992 York 1985. 84S. 45.6 t.
**TSO.** Dia. EH224. Lot No. 30993 York 1985. 84S. 27.1 t.
**TSO n.** Dia. EH224. Lot No. 30932 Derby 1981. 84S. 27.1 t.

\* – Chopper control. § – Tread brakes.
c TSO have "Crossrail" interiors.

| 5901 |   | N | NSBX | WD | 77813 62826 71714 77814 |
|------|---|---|------|----|--------------------------|
| 5902 |   | N | NSBX | WD | 77815 62827 71715 77816 |
| 5903 |   | N | NSBX | WD | 77817 62828 71716 77818 |
| 5904 |   | N | NSBX | WD | 77819 62829 71717 77820 |
| 5905 |   | N | NSBX | WD | 77821 62830 71718 77822 |
| 5906 |   | N | NSBX | WD | 77823 62831 71719 77824 |
| 5907 |   | N | NSBX | WD | 77825 62832 71720 77826 |
| 5908 |   | N | NSBX | WD | 77827 62833 71721 77828 |
| 5909 |   | N | NSBX | WD | 77829 62834 71722 77830 |
| 5910 |   | N | NSBX | WD | 77831 62835 71723 77832 |
| 5911 |   | N | NSBX | WD | 77833 62836 71724 77834 |
| 5912 | \* | N | NSBX | WD | 77835 62837 71725 77836 |
| 5913 | § | N | NSBX | WD | 77837 62838 71726 77838 |
| 5914 | § | N | NSBX | WD | 77839 62839 71727 77840 |
| 5915 | § | N | NSBX | WD | 77841 62840 71728 77842 |
| 5916 | \* | N | NSBX | WD | 77843 62841 71729 77844 |
| 5917 | \* | N | NSBX | WD | 77845 62842 71730 77846 |
| 5918 | \*c | N | NSBX | WD | 77847 62843 71731 77848 |
| 5919 | \*c | N | NSBX | WD | 77849 62844 71732 77850 |
| 5920 | \* | N | NSBX | WD | 77851 62845 71733 77852 |

# CLASS 416/2         BR DESIGN 2 EPB

DMBSO – DTSso.

**Electrical Equipment:** 1951-type.
**Bogies:** Mk. 3D.
**Gangways:** Non-gangwayed.
**Traction Motors:** Two EE507 of 185 kW.
**Dimensions:** 19.49 x 2.82 m.
**Maximum Speed:** 75 mph.

**65301 – 65304. DMBSO.** Dia. EB269. Lot No. 30114 Ashford/Eastleigh 1954.
84S. 42 t.
**65327 – 65341. DMBSO.** Dia. EB269. Lot No. 30119 Ashford/Eastleigh 1954.
84S. 42 t.

**65344 – 65365. DMBSO**. Dia. EB269. Lot No. 30167 Ashford/Eastleigh 1955. 84S. 42 t.
**65367 – 65392. DMBSO**. Dia. EB269. Lot No. 30314 Ashford/Eastleigh 1956 – 58. 84S. 42 t.
**77501 – 77504. DTSso**. Dia. EE264. Lot No. 30115 Ashford/Eastleigh 1954. 102S. 30.5 t.
**77512 – 77526. DTSso**. Dia. EE264. Lot No. 30120 Ashford/Eastleigh 1954. 102S. 30.5 t.
**77529 – 77550. DTSso**. Dia. EE264. Lot No. 30168 Ashford/Eastleigh 1955. 102S. 30.5 t.
**77552 – 77577. DTSso**. Dia. EE264. Lot No. 30315 Ashford/Eastleigh 1956 – 58. 102S. 30.5 t.

Note: 77537/9 are DTSO and seat 92S. (Dia. EE275).

| | | | | |
|---|---|---|---|---|
| 6202 | NKSX | SG | 65301 | 77501 |
| 6203 | NKSX | SG | 65302 | 77502 |
| 6205 | NKSX | SG | 65304 | 77504 |
| 6213 | NKSX | SG | 65327 | 77512 |
| 6217 | NKSX | SG | 65331 | 77516 |
| 6221 | NKSX | SG | 65335 | 77520 |
| 6223 | NKSX | SG | 65337 | 77522 |
| 6224 | NKSX | SG | 65338 | 77523 |
| 6225 | NKSX | SG | 65339 | 77524 |
| 6226 | NKSX | SG | 65340 | 77525 |
| 6227 | NKSX | SG | 65341 | 77526 |
| 6230 | NKSX | SG | 65344 | 77529 |
| 6231 | NKSX | SG | 65345 | 77530 |
| 6235 | NKSX | SG | 65349 | 77534 |
| 6236 | NKSX | SG | 65350 | 77535 |
| 6237 | NKSX | SG | 65351 | 77536 |
| 6239 | NKSX | SG | 65353 | 77538 |
| 6240 | NKSX | SG | 65354 | 77539 |
| 6241 | NKSX | SG | 65355 | 77540 |
| 6245 | NKSX | SG | 65359 | 77544 |
| 6247 | NKSX | SG | 65361 | 77546 |
| 6249 | NKSX | SG | 65363 | 77548 |
| 6251 | NKSX | SG | 65365 | 77550 |
| 6253 | NKSX | SG | 65367 | 77552 |
| 6255 | NKSX | SG | 65369 | 77554 |
| 6256 | NKSX | SG | 65370 | 77555 |
| 6259 | NKSX | SG | 65373 | 77558 |
| 6260 | NKSX | SG | 65374 | 77559 |
| 6261 | NKSX | SG | 65375 | 77560 |
| 6262 | NKSX | SG | 65376 | 77561 |
| 6263 | NKSX | SG | 65377 | 77562 |
| 6264 | NKSX | SG | 65378 | 77563 |
| 6265 | NKSX | SG | 65379 | 77564 |
| 6267 | NKSX | SG | 65381 | 77566 |
| 6268 | NKSX | SG | 65382 | 77567 |
| 6270 | NKSX | SG | 65384 | 77569 |
| 6271 | NKSX | SG | 65385 | 77570 |
| 6272 | NKSX | SG | 65386 | 77571 |

| 6273 | NKSX | SG | 65387 77572 |
|---|---|---|---|
| 6274 | NKSX | SG | 65388 77573 |
| 6275 | NKSX | SG | 65389 77574 |
| 6277 | NKSX | SG (S) | 65391 77576 |
| 6278 | NKSX | SG | 65392 77577 |

# CLASS 416/3                              SR DESIGN 2 EPB

DMBSO – DTSso. These units were made by producing new bodies for former 2 Nol underframes. All have now been facelifted with new seat trim, fluorescent lighting and PA.

**Electrical Equipment:** 1951-type.
**Bogies:** Central 40'' motor bogies and SR standard trailer bogies.
**Gangways:** Non-gangwayed.
**Traction Motors:** Two EE507 of 185 kW.
**Dimensions:** 19.05 x 2.82 m.
**Maximum Speed:** 75 mph.

**14283. DMBSO.** Dia. EB269. Lot No. 4016 Eastleigh 1954 – 5. 82S. 40 t.
**14542 – 14590. DMBSO.** Dia. EB269. Lot No. 4281 Eastleigh 1957 – 9. 82S. 40 t.
**DTSO.** Dia. EE269. Lot No. 4281 Eastleigh 1957 – 9. 92S. 30 t.

| 6301 | N | NSLX | SU | 14577 16121 |
|---|---|---|---|---|
| 6302 | N | NSLX | SU | 14580 16124 |
| 6303 | N | NSLX | SU | 14576 16120 |
| 6304 | N | NSLX | SU | 14589 16133 |
| 6305 | N | NSLX | SU | 14587 16131 |
| 6306 | N | NSLX | SU | 14571 16115 |
| 6307 | N | NSLX | SU | 14573 16117 |
| 6308 | N | NSLX | SU | 14564 16108 |
| 6309 | N | NSLX | SU | 14562 16106 |
| 6310 | N | NSLX | SU | 14574 16118 |
| 6311 | N | NSLX | SU | 14565 16109 |
| 6312 | N | NSLX | SU | 14579 16123 |
| 6313 | N | NSLX | SU | 14558 16102 |
| 6314 | N | NSLX | SU | 14586 16130 |
| 6315 | N | NSLX | SU | 14590 16134 |
| 6316 | N | NSLX | SU | 14559 16103 |
| 6317 | N | NSLX | SU | 14578 16122 |
| 6318 | N | NSLX | SU | 14566 16110 |
| 6319 | N | NSLX | SU | 14568 16112 |
| 6320 | N | NSLX | SU | 14561 16105 |
| 6321 | N | NSLX | SU | 14283 16128 |
| 6322 | N | NSLX | SU | 14488 16119 |
| 6323 | N | NSLX | SU | 14581 16125 |
| 6324 | N | NSLX | SU | 14560 16104 |
| 6325 | N | NSLX | SU | 14567 16111 |
| 6326 | N | NSLX | SU | 14585 16129 |
| 6327 | N | NSLX | SU | 14572 16116 |
| 6328 | N | NSLX | SU | 14582 16126 |
| 6329 | N | NSLX | SU | 14542 16114 |

| 6330 | N | NSLX | SU | 14588 16132 |
|------|---|------|----|-----|
| 6331 | N | NSLX | SU | 14583 16127 |
| 6332 |   | NSLX | SU | 14569 16113 |
| 6333 | N | NSLX | SU | 14557 16101 |
| 6334 | N | NSLX | SU | 14546 16107 |

# CLASS 416/4      FACELIFTED BR DESIGN 2 EPB

DMBSO – DTSO. Facelifted units with new trim, fluorescent lighting and PA.

**Electrical Equipment:** 1951-type.
**Bogies:** Mk. 3D.
**Gangways:** Non-gangwayed.
**Traction Motors:** Two EE507 of 185 kW.
**Dimensions:** 19.49 x 2.82 m.
**Maximum Speed:** 75 mph.

**65305 – 65309. DMBSO.** Dia. EB281. Lot No. 30114 Ashford/Eastleigh 1954. 82S. 42 t.
**65328 – 65334. DMBSO.** Dia. EB281. Lot No. 30119 Ashford/Eastleigh 1954. 82S. 42 t.
**65342 – 65366. DMBSO.** Dia. EB281. Lot No. 30167 Ashford/Eastleigh 1955. 82S. 42 t.
**65368 – 65372. DMBSO.** Dia. EB281. Lot No. 30314 Ashford/Eastleigh 1956 – 58. 79S. 42 t.
**77113. DTSO.** Dia. EE279. Lot No. 30117 Eastleigh 1955. Former South Tyneside trailer. 92s. 30.5 t.
**77505. DTSO.** Dia. EE274. Lot No. 30115 Ashford/Eastleigh 1954. 92S. 30.5 t.
**77513 – 77519. DTSO.** Dia. EE274. Lot No. 30120 Ashford/Eastleigh 1954. 92S. 30.5 t.
**77527 – 77551. DTSO.** Dia. EE274. Lot No. 30168 Ashford/Eastleigh 1955. 92S. 30.5 t.
**77553 – 77557. DTSO.** Dia. EE274. Lot No. 30315 Ashford/Eastleigh 1956 – 58. 92S. 30.5 t.

\* – Modified for working Maidstone service. Doors fitted between saloon and guards compartment in motor car and between saloon and cab in trailer. DMBSO seats 79S (dia. EB280) and DTSO seats 90S (dia. EE271).

| 6401 | * | N | NKSX | SG | 65346 77531 |
|------|---|---|------|----|-----|
| 6402 | * | N | NKSX | SG | 65362 77547 |
| 6403 | * | N | NKSX | SG | 65356 77541 |
| 6404 | * | N | NKSX | SG | 65329 77514 |
| 6405 | * | N | NKSX | SG | 65347 77532 |
| 6406 | * | N | NKSX | SG | 65305 77505 |
| 6407 | * | N | NKSX | SG | 65330 77515 |
| 6408 | * | N | NKSX | SG | 65342 77527 |
| 6409 | * | N | NKSX | SG | 65309 77113 |
| 6410 |   | N | NKSX | SG | 65334 77519 |
| 6411 |   | N | NKSX | SG | 65333 77518 |
| 6412 |   | N | NKSX | SG | 65364 77549 |
| 6413 |   | N | NKSX | SG | 65372 77557 |
| 6414 |   | N | NKSX | SG | 65368 77553 |
| 6415 |   | N | NKSX | SG | 65348 77533 |

| 6416 | N | NKSX | SG | 65328 | 77513 |
|------|---|------|----|-------|-------|
| 6417 | N | NKSX | SG | 65366 | 77551 |
| 6418 | N | NKSX | SG | 65360 | 77545 |

## CLASS 488  VICTORIA – GATWICK TRAILER SETS

TFOLH – TSOL (Class 488/3 only) – TSOLH. Converted 1983 – 84 from loco-hauled Mk. 2F FOs and TSOs for Victoria – Gatwick service. Express stock. Air conditioned. Fluorescent lighting. PA. Conversion consisted of a modified seating layout and the removal of one toilet to provide additional luggage space.

**Bogies:** B4.
**Gangways:** Throughout.
**Dimensions:** 20.12 x 2.82 m.
**Maximum Speed:** 90 mph.

**72500 – 72509. TFOLH.** Dia. EP101. Lot No. 30859 Derby 1973 – 74. 41F 1L. 35 t.
**72602 – 72647. TSOLH.** Dia. EP201. Lot No. 30860 Derby 1973 – 74. 48S 1L. 35 t.
**72701 – 72718. TSOL.** Dia. EH285. Lot No. 30860 Derby 1973 – 74. 48S 1L. 35 t.

**CLASS 488/2.** Note: TFOLH fitted with public telephone.

| 8201 | I | IVGX | SL | 72500 (3413) | 72638 (6068) |
|------|---|------|----|--------------|--------------|
| 8202 | I | IVGX | SL | 72501 (3382) | 72617 (6086) |
| 8203 | I | IVGX | SL | 72502 (3321) | 72640 (6097) |
| 8204 | I | IVGX | SL | 72503 (3407) | 72641 (6079) |
| 8205 | I | IVGX | SL | 72504 (3406) | 72628 (6058) |
| 8206 | I | IVGX | SL | 72505 (3415) | 72629 (6048) |
| 8207 | I | IVGX | SL | 72506 (3335) | 72642 (6076) |
| 8208 | I | IVGX | SL | 72507 (3412) | 72643 (6040) |
| 8209 | I | IVGX | SL | 72508 (3409) | 72644 (6039) |
| 8210 | I | IVGX | SL | 72509 (3398) | 72635 (6128) |

**CLASS 488/3.** TSOLH – TSOL – TSOLH.

| 8302 | I | IVGX | SL | 72602 (6130) | 72701 (6088) | 72604 (6087) |
|------|---|------|----|--------------|--------------|--------------|
| 8303 | I | IVGX | SL | 72603 (6093) | 72702 (6099) | 72608 (6077) |
| 8304 | I | IVGX | SL | 72606 (6084) | 72703 (6075) | 72611 (6083) |
| 8305 | I | IVGX | SL | 72605 (6082) | 72704 (6132) | 72609 (6080) |
| 8306 | I | IVGX | SL | 72607 (6020) | 72705 (6032) | 72610 (6074) |
| 8307 | I | IVGX | SL | 72612 (6156) | 72706 (6143) | 72613 (6126) |
| 8308 | I | IVGX | SL | 72614 (6090) | 72707 (6127) | 72615 (5938) |
| 8309 | I | IVGX | SL | 72616 (6007) | 72708 (6095) | 72639 (6070) |
| 8310 | I | IVGX | SL | 72618 (6044) | 72709 (5982) | 72619 (5909) |
| 8311 | I | IVGX | SL | 72620 (6140) | 72710 (6003) | 72621 (6108) |
| 8312 | I | IVGX | SL | 72622 (6004) | 72711 (6109) | 72623 (6118) |
| 8313 | I | IVGX | SL | 72624 (5972) | 72712 (6091) | 72625 (6085) |
| 8314 | I | IVGX | SL | 72626 (6017) | 72713 (6023) | 72627 (5974) |
| 8315 | I | IVGX | SL | 72636 (6071) | 72714 (6092) | 72645 (5942) |
| 8316 | I | IVGX | SL | 72630 (6094) | 72715 (6019) | 72631 (6096) |
| 8317 | I | IVGX | SL | 72632 (6072) | 72716 (6114) | 72633 (6129) |
| 8318 | I | IVGX | SL | 72634 (6089) | 72717 (6069) | 72637 (6098) |
| 8319 | I | IVGX | SL | 72646 (6078) | 72718 (5979) | 72647 (6081) |

## CLASS 489             VICTORIA – GATWICK GLV

Converted 1983 – 84 from class 414/3 (2 Hap) DMBSOs to work with class 488. **Bogies:** Mk 4.
**Gangways:** Gangwayed at inner end only.
**Traction Motors:** Two EE507 of 185 kW.
**Dimensions:** 19.49 x 2.82 m.
**Maximum Speed:** 90 mph.

**DMLV.** Dia. EX561. Lot No. 30452 Ashford/Eastleigh 1959. 40.5 t.

| | | | | | | | |
|---|---|---|---|---|---|---|---|
| 9101 | I | IVGX SL | 68500 (61269) | 9106 | I | IVGX SL | 68505 (61299) |
| 9102 | I | IVGX SL | 68501 (61281) | 9107 | I | IVGX SL | 68506 (61292) |
| 9103 | I | IVGX SL | 68502 (61274) | 9108 | I | IVGX SL | 68507 (61267) |
| 9104 | I | IVGX SL | 68503 (61277) | 9109 | I | IVGX SL | 68508 (61272) |
| 9105 | I | IVGX SL | 68504 (61286) | 9110 | I | IVGX SL | 68509 (61280) |

## CLASS 456

DMSO – DTSO. Sliding doors. Disc brakes. Fluorescent lighting. PA.

**Bogies:** P7 (motor) and T3 trailer.
**Gangways:** Within set.
**Traction Motors:** Two EE507 of 185 kW.
**Dimensions:** 19.83 x 2.82 m.
**Maximum Speed:** 75 mph.

**DMSO.** Dia. EA267. Lot No. 31073 York 1990 – 1. 79S. 41.1 t.
**DTSO.** Dia. EE276. Lot No. 31074 York 1990 – 1. 51S. 31.4 t.

| | | | | |
|---|---|---|---|---|
| 456 001 | N | NSLX | SU | 64735 78250 |
| 456 002 | N | NSLX | SU | 64736 78251 |
| 456 003 | N | NSLX | SU | 64737 78252 |
| 456 004 | N | NSLX | SU | 64738 78253 |
| 456 005 | N | NSLX | SU | 64739 78254 |
| 456 006 | N | NSLX | SU | 64740 78255 |
| 456 007 | N | NSLX | SU | 64741 78256 |
| 456 008 | N | NSLX | SU | 64742 78257 |
| 456 009 | N | NSLX | SU | 64743 78258 |
| 456 010 | N | NSLX | SU | 64744 78259 |
| 456 011 | N | NSLX | SU | 64745 78260 |
| 456 012 | N | NSLX | SU | 64746 78261 |
| 456 013 | N | NSLX | SU | 64747 78262 |
| 456 014 | N | NSLX | SU | 64748 78263 |
| 456 015 | N | NSLX | SU | 64749 78264 |
| 456 016 | N | NSLX | SU | 64750 78265 |
| 456 017 | N | NSLX | SU | 64751 78266 |
| 456 018 | N | NSLX | SU | 64752 78267 |
| 456 019 | N | NSLX | SU | 64753 78268 |
| 456 020 | N | NSLX | SU | 64754 78269 |
| 456 021 | N | NSLX | SU | 64755 78270 |

| | | | | | |
|---|---|---|---|---|---|
| 456 022 | N | NSLX | SU | 64756 | 78271 |
| 456 023 | N | NSLX | SU | 64757 | 78272 |
| 456 024 | N | NSLX | SU | 64758 | 78273 |

# CLASS 465 NETWORKER

DMSO – TSO – TSOL – DMSO. New units with Aluminium bodies. Sliding doors. Disc, rheostatic and regenerative brakes. PA.

**Electrical Equipment:** Networker.
**Bogies:**
**Gangways:** Within set.
**Traction Motors:**
**Dimensions:**
**Maximum Speed:** 75 mph.

**64759 – 64808. DMSO(A).** Dia. EA268. Lot No. 31100 BREL York 1991 – 2. 86S. t.
**64809 – 64858. DMSO(B).** Dia. EA268. Lot No. 31100 BREL York 1991 – 2. 86S. t.
**65700 – 65749. DMSO(A).** Dia. EA269. Lot No. 31103 Metro-Cammell 1991 – 2. 86S. t.
**65750 – 65799. DMSO(B).** Dia. EA269. Lot No. 31103 Metro-Cammell 1991 – 2. 86S. t.
**72028 – 72126 (even Nos.). TSO.** Dia. EH293. Lot No. 31102 BREL York 1991 – 2. 86S. t.
**72029 – 72127 (odd Nos.). TSOL.** Dia. EH292. Lot No. 31101 BREL York 1991 – 2. 86S. t.
**72719 – 72817 (odd Nos.). TSOL.** Dia. EH294. Lot No. 31104 Metro-Cammell 1991 – 2. 86S. t.
**72720 – 72818 (even Nos.). TSO.** Dia. EH295. Lot No. 31105 Metro-Cammell 1991 – 2. 86S. t.

**Class 465/0. Built by BREL Ltd.**

| | | | | | | | |
|---|---|---|---|---|---|---|---|
| 465 001 | N | NKSX | SG | 64759 | 72028 | 72029 | 64809 |
| 465 002 | N | NKSX | SG | 64760 | 72030 | 72031 | 64810 |
| 465 003 | N | NKSX | SG | 64761 | 72032 | 72033 | 64811 |
| 465 004 | N | NKSX | SG | 64762 | 72034 | 72035 | 64812 |
| 465 005 | N | NKSX | SG | 64763 | 72036 | 72037 | 64813 |
| 465 006 | N | NKSX | SG | 64764 | 72038 | 72039 | 64814 |
| 465 007 | N | NKSX | SG | 64765 | 72040 | 72041 | 64815 |
| 465 008 | N | NKSX | SG | 64766 | 72042 | 72043 | 64816 |
| 465 009 | N | NKSX | | 64767 | 72044 | 72045 | 64817 |
| 465 010 | N | NKSX | | 64768 | 72046 | 72047 | 64818 |
| 465 011 | N | NKSX | | 64769 | 72048 | 72049 | 64819 |
| 465 012 | N | NKSX | | 64770 | 72050 | 72051 | 64820 |
| 465 013 | N | NKSX | | 64771 | 72052 | 72053 | 64821 |
| 465 014 | N | NKSX | | 64772 | 72054 | 72055 | 64822 |
| 465 015 | N | NKSX | | 64773 | 72056 | 72057 | 64823 |
| 465 016 | N | NKSX | | 64774 | 72058 | 72059 | 64824 |
| 465 017 | N | NKSX | | 64775 | 72060 | 72061 | 64825 |
| 465 018 | N | NKSX | | 64776 | 72062 | 72063 | 64826 |
| 465 019 | N | NKSX | | 64777 | 72064 | 72065 | 64827 |

▲ Class 421/5 ('Greyhound 4 Cig') unit No. 1312 stands at Portsmouth Harbour on 29th August 1992.
*Mervyn Turvey*

▼ Refurbished Class 412 (4 Bep) unit No. 2305 forms the front portion of the
11.05 Portsmouth Harbour – Waterloo at Fratton on 3rd April 1992.
*Brian Denton*

Class 442 (Wessex Electric) units Nos. 2406 & 2424 form the 0706 Portsmouth Harbour – Waterloo at Portcreek Junction on 16th May 1992.

▲ Class 413/4 (4 Cap) No. 3321 approaches Orpington whilst forming the 12.38 from Victoria on 8th September 1992. *Chris Wilson*

▼ Class 423 (4 Vep) No. 3405 near Southampton with the 13.05 Waterloo – Southampton on 12th September 1992. *Chris Wilson*

▲ SR design Class 415/4 (4 EPB) No. 5486 with one blue and grey MBSO stand at Woolwich Arsenal with the 14.57 Charing Cross – Gillingham on 8th September 1992.                                                                    *Chris Wilson*

▼ Class 455/7 No. 5702 leaves Wimbledon on 27th July 1992 with a Guildford train.                                                                                            *Hugh Ballantyne*

SR design Class 416/3 2 EPB No. 6301 forms the front portion of the 10.10 Victoria – East Grinstead at Clapham cutting on 27th March 1991.

*Brain Denton*

Class 456 No. 456 011 approaching Clapham Junction on 27th July 1992.

*Hugh Ballantyne*

Class 456 No. 465 001 arrives at Fulwell with a Shepperton to Strawberry Hill test trip on 6th March 1992.

Isle of Wight Class 483 units Nos. 483 004 & 438 008 leave Ryde Pier Head with a Shanklin service on 31st July 1992.

*John Augustson*

▲ Class 507 No. 507 005 pauses at Kirkdale on 13th October 1992 with Kirkby service.　　　　　　　　　　　　　　　　　　*Norman Barrington*

▼ Class 508 No. 508 134 arrives at Kirkdale with a Liverpool Central servic on 19th June 1992.　　　　　　　　　　　　　　　*Hugh Ballantyn*

| | | | | | | | |
|---|---|---|---|---|---|---|---|
| 465 020 | N | NKSX | | 64778 | 72066 | 72067 | 64828 |
| 465 021 | N | NKSX | | 64779 | 72068 | 72069 | 64829 |
| 465 022 | N | NKSX | | 64780 | 72070 | 72071 | 64830 |
| 465 023 | N | NKSX | | 64781 | 72072 | 72073 | 64831 |
| 465 024 | N | NKSX | | 64782 | 72074 | 72075 | 64832 |
| 465 025 | N | NKSX | | 64783 | 72076 | 72077 | 64833 |
| 465 026 | N | NKSX | | 64784 | 72078 | 72079 | 64834 |
| 465 027 | N | NKSX | | 64785 | 72080 | 72081 | 64835 |
| 465 028 | N | NKSX | | 64786 | 72082 | 72083 | 64836 |
| 465 029 | N | NKSX | | 64787 | 72084 | 72085 | 64837 |
| 465 030 | N | NKSX | | 64788 | 72086 | 72087 | 64838 |
| 465 031 | N | NKSX | | 64789 | 72088 | 72089 | 64839 |
| 465 032 | N | NKSX | | 64790 | 72090 | 72091 | 64840 |
| 465 033 | N | NKSX | | 64791 | 72092 | 72093 | 64841 |
| 465 034 | N | NKSX | | 64792 | 72094 | 72095 | 64842 |
| 465 035 | N | NKSX | | 64793 | 72096 | 72097 | 64843 |
| 465 036 | N | NKSX | | 64794 | 72098 | 72099 | 64844 |
| 465 037 | N | NKSX | | 64795 | 72100 | 72101 | 64845 |
| 465 038 | N | NKSX | | 64796 | 72102 | 72103 | 64846 |
| 465 039 | N | NKSX | | 64797 | 72104 | 72105 | 64847 |
| 465 040 | N | NKSX | | 64798 | 72106 | 72107 | 64848 |
| 465 041 | N | NKSX | | 64799 | 72108 | 72109 | 64849 |
| 465 042 | N | NKSX | | 64800 | 72110 | 72111 | 64850 |
| 465 043 | N | NKSX | | 64801 | 72112 | 72113 | 64851 |
| 465 044 | N | NKSX | | 64802 | 72114 | 72115 | 64852 |
| 465 045 | N | NKSX | | 64803 | 72116 | 72117 | 64853 |
| 465 046 | N | NKSX | | 64804 | 72118 | 72119 | 64854 |
| 465 047 | N | NKSX | | 64805 | 72120 | 72121 | 64855 |
| 465 048 | N | NKSX | | 64806 | 72122 | 72123 | 64856 |
| 465 049 | N | NKSX | | 64807 | 72124 | 72125 | 64857 |
| 465 050 | N | NKSX | | 64808 | 72126 | 72127 | 64858 |

## Class 465/2. Built by Metro-Cammell.

| | | | | | | | |
|---|---|---|---|---|---|---|---|
| 465 201 | N | NKSX | SG | 65700 | 72719 | 72720 | 65750 |
| 465 202 | N | NKSX | SG | 65701 | 72721 | 72722 | 65751 |
| 465 203 | N | NKSX | SG | 65702 | 72723 | 72724 | 65752 |
| 465 204 | N | NKSX | SG | 65703 | 72725 | 72726 | 65753 |
| 465 205 | N | NKSX | SG | 65704 | 72727 | 72728 | 65754 |
| 465 206 | N | NKSX | SG | 65705 | 72729 | 72730 | 65755 |
| 465 207 | N | NKSX | SG | 65706 | 72731 | 72732 | 65756 |
| 465 208 | N | NKSX | SG | 65707 | 72733 | 72734 | 65757 |
| 465 209 | N | NKSX | SG | 65708 | 72735 | 72736 | 65758 |
| 465 210 | N | NKSX | SG | 65709 | 72737 | 72738 | 65759 |
| 465 211 | N | NKSX | SG | 65710 | 72739 | 72740 | 65760 |
| 465 212 | N | NKSX | SG | 65711 | 72741 | 72742 | 65761 |
| 465 213 | N | NKSX | SG | 65712 | 72743 | 72744 | 65762 |
| 465 214 | N | NKSX | SG | 65713 | 72745 | 72746 | 65763 |
| 465 215 | N | NKSX | SG | 65714 | 72747 | 72748 | 65764 |
| 465 216 | N | NKSX | SG | 65715 | 72749 | 72750 | 65765 |
| 465 217 | N | NKSX | SG | 65716 | 72751 | 72752 | 65766 |
| 465 218 | N | NKSX | SG | 65717 | 72753 | 72754 | 65767 |
| 465 219 | N | NKSX | SG | 65718 | 72755 | 72756 | 65768 |

| | | | | | | | |
|---|---|---|---|---|---|---|---|
| 465 220 | N | NKSX | SG | 65719 | 72757 | 72758 | 65769 |
| 465 221 | N | NKSX | | 65720 | 72759 | 72760 | 65770 |
| 465 222 | N | NKSX | | 65721 | 72761 | 72762 | 65771 |
| 465 223 | N | NKSX | | 65722 | 72763 | 72764 | 65772 |
| 465 224 | N | NKSX | | 65723 | 72765 | 72766 | 65773 |
| 465 225 | N | NKSX | | 65724 | 72767 | 72768 | 65774 |
| 465 226 | N | NKSX | | 65725 | 72769 | 72770 | 65775 |
| 465 227 | N | NKSX | | 65726 | 72771 | 72772 | 65776 |
| 465 228 | N | NKSX | | 65727 | 72773 | 72774 | 65777 |
| 465 229 | N | NKSX | | 65728 | 72775 | 72776 | 65778 |
| 465 230 | N | NKSX | | 65729 | 72777 | 72778 | 65779 |
| 465 231 | N | NKSX | | 65730 | 72779 | 72780 | 65780 |
| 465 232 | N | NKSX | | 65731 | 72781 | 72782 | 65781 |
| 465 233 | N | NKSX | | 65732 | 72783 | 72784 | 65782 |
| 465 234 | N | NKSX | | 65733 | 72785 | 72786 | 65783 |
| 465 235 | N | NKSX | | 65734 | 72787 | 72788 | 65784 |
| 465 236 | N | NKSX | | 65735 | 72789 | 72790 | 65785 |
| 465 237 | N | NKSX | | 65736 | 72791 | 72792 | 65786 |
| 465 238 | N | NKSX | | 65737 | 72793 | 72794 | 65787 |
| 465 239 | N | NKSX | | 65738 | 72795 | 72796 | 65788 |
| 465 240 | N | NKSX | | 65739 | 72797 | 72798 | 65789 |
| 465 241 | N | NKSX | | 65740 | 72799 | 72800 | 65790 |
| 465 242 | N | NKSX | | 65741 | 72801 | 72802 | 65791 |
| 465 243 | N | NKSX | | 65742 | 72803 | 72804 | 65792 |
| 465 244 | N | NKSX | | 65743 | 72805 | 72806 | 65793 |
| 465 245 | N | NKSX | | 65744 | 72807 | 72808 | 65794 |
| 465 246 | N | NKSX | | 65745 | 72809 | 72810 | 65795 |
| 465 247 | N | NKSX | | 65746 | 72811 | 72812 | 65796 |
| 465 248 | N | NKSX | | 65747 | 72813 | 72814 | 65797 |
| 465 249 | N | NKSX | | 65748 | 72815 | 72816 | 65798 |
| 465 250 | N | NKSX | | 65749 | 72817 | 72818 | 65799 |

# CLASS 466 NETWORKER

DMSO – DTSO. New units with Aluminium bodies. Sliding doors. Disc, rheostatic and regenerative brakes. PA.

**Electrical Equipment:** Networker.
**Bogies:**
**Gangways:** Within set.
**Traction Motors:**
**Dimensions:**
**Maximum Speed:** 75 mph.

**DMSO.** Dia. EA2 . Lot No. 31128 Metro-Cammell 1992 – 3. 86S.    t.
**DTSO.** Dia. EE277. Lot No. 31129 Metro-Cammell 1991 – 2. 82S.    t.

| | | | | |
|---|---|---|---|---|
| 466 001 | N | NKSX | 64860 | 78312 |
| 466 002 | N | NKSX | 64861 | 78313 |
| 466 003 | N | NKSX | 64862 | 78314 |
| 466 004 | N | NKSX | 64863 | 78315 |
| 466 005 | N | NKSX | 64864 | 78316 |
| 466 006 | N | NKSX | 64865 | 78317 |

| | | | | | |
|---|---|---|---|---|---|
| 466 007 | **N** | NKSX | 64866 | 78318 |
| 466 008 | **N** | NKSX | 64867 | 78319 |
| 466 009 | **N** | NKSX | 64868 | 78320 |
| 466 010 | **N** | NKSX | 64869 | 78321 |
| 466 011 | **N** | NKSX | 64870 | 78322 |
| 466 012 | **N** | NKSX | 64871 | 78323 |
| 466 013 | **N** | NKSX | 64872 | 78324 |
| 466 014 | **N** | NKSX | 64873 | 78325 |
| 466 015 | **N** | NKSX | 64874 | 78326 |
| 466 016 | **N** | NKSX | 64875 | 78327 |
| 466 017 | **N** | NKSX | 64876 | 78328 |
| 466 018 | **N** | NKSX | 64877 | 78329 |
| 466 019 | **N** | NKSX | 64878 | 78330 |
| 466 020 | **N** | NKSX | 64879 | 78331 |
| 466 021 | **N** | NKSX | 64880 | 78332 |
| 466 022 | **N** | NKSX | 64881 | 78333 |
| 466 023 | **N** | NKSX | 64882 | 78334 |
| 466 024 | **N** | NKSX | 64883 | 78335 |
| 466 025 | **N** | NKSX | 64884 | 78336 |
| 466 026 | **N** | NKSX | 64885 | 78337 |
| 466 027 | **N** | NKSX | 64886 | 78338 |
| 466 028 | **N** | NKSX | 64887 | 78339 |
| 466 029 | **N** | NKSX | 64888 | 78340 |
| 466 030 | **N** | NKSX | 64889 | 78341 |
| 466 031 | **N** | NKSX | 64890 | 78342 |
| 466 032 | **N** | NKSX | 64891 | 78343 |
| 466 033 | **N** | NKSX | 64892 | 78344 |
| 466 034 | **N** | NKSX | 64893 | 78345 |
| 466 035 | **N** | NKSX | 64894 | 78346 |
| 466 036 | **N** | NKSX | 64895 | 78347 |
| 466 037 | **N** | NKSX | 64896 | 78348 |
| 466 038 | **N** | NKSX | 64897 | 78349 |
| 466 039 | **N** | NKSX | 64898 | 78350 |
| 466 040 | **N** | NKSX | 64899 | 78351 |
| 466 041 | **N** | NKSX | 64900 | 78352 |
| 466 042 | **N** | NKSX | 64901 | 78353 |
| 466 043 | **N** | NKSX | 64902 | 78354 |

# SOUTHERN REGION TUBE STOCK

These classes are tube stock used on the Isle of Wight or for the Waterloo and City line in London (known colloquially as the "Drain").

## CLASS 483        'NEW' ISLE OF WIGHT STOCK

DMBSO(A) – DMBSO(B). Built 19    for LTE. Converted 1989 – 90 for Isle of Wight Line. Sliding doors. End doors. dg. pa. Former London Underground numbers are shown in parentheses.

**System:** 660 V d.c. third rail.
**Gangways:** Non-gangwayed.
**Traction Motors:** Two of 130 kW.
**Dimensions:** 15.95 x 2.69 m.
**Maximum Speed:** 45 mph.

**DMSO (A).** Lot No. 31071. Dia. EA265. 42S. 27.5 t.
**DMSO (B).** Lot No. 31072. Dia. EA266. 42S. 27.5 t.

| 483 001 | N | NSSX | RY | 121 | (10184) | 221 | (11184) |
|---------|---|------|----|-----|---------|-----|---------|
| 483 002 | N | NSSX | RY | 122 | (10221) | 222 | (11221) |
| 483 003 | N | NSSX | RY | 123 | (10116) | 223 | (11116) |
| 483 004 | N | NSSX | RY | 124 | (10205) | 224 | (11205) |
| 483 005 | N | NSSX | RY | 125 | (10142) | 225 | (11142) |
| 483 006 | N | NSSX | RY | 126 | (10297) | 226 | (11297) |
| 483 007 | N | NSSX | RY | 127 | (10291) | 227 | (11291) |
| 483 008 | N | NSSX | RY | 128 | (10255) | 228 | (11255) |
| 483 009 | N | NSSX | RY | 129 | (10289) | 229 | (11229) |

## CLASSES 485 & 486       ISLE OF WIGHT STOCK

DMBSO – 2TSO – DTSO. Built 1923 – 31 for London Electric Railway (later LT). Converted 1967 for Isle of Wight Line. Sliding doors. End doors. Former London Underground numbers are shown in parentheses. Deicing unit.

**System:** 660 V d.c. third rail.
**Gangways:** Non-gangwayed.
**Traction Motors:** Two EE507 of 178 kW.
**Dimensions:** 15.16 x 2.64 m.
**Maximum Speed:** 45 mph.

**DMBSO.** Dia. EB261. Metro-Cammell 1932 – 5. 26S. 32 t.
**TSO.** Dia. EH261. Cammell-Laird 1924. 42S. 19 t.
**DTSO.** Dia. EE260. Metro-Cammell 1926 – 9. 38S. 17 t.

| 485 | | N | NXXZ | RY | 5 | (3185) | 31 | (5283) | 28 | (5304) |
|-----|---|---|------|----|---|--------|----|--------|----|--------|

## CLASS 487        WATERLOO & CITY

Built 1940. Do not run in permanent sets. Run as single motor cars or as pairs of motors with up to three trailers in between.

**System:** 630 V d.c. third rail.
**Gangways:** Non-gangwayed. End doors.
**Traction Motors:** Two EE500 of 140 kW.
**Dimensions:** 14.33 x 2.64 m.
**Maximum Speed:** 35 mph.

**DMBSO.** Dia. EB260. English Electric 1940. 40S. 29 t.
**TSO.** Dia. EH260. English Electric 1940. 52S. 19 t.

### DMBSO

| | | | | | | | | | | |
|---|---|---|---|---|---|---|---|---|---|---|
| 51 | **N** | NKSX | WC | 56 | **N** | NKSX | WC | 60 | **N** | NKSX | WC |
| 53 | **N** | NKSX | WC | 57 | **N** | NKSX | WC | 61 | **N** | NKSX | WC |
| 54 | **N** | NKSX | WC | 58 | **N** | NKSX | WC | 62 | **N** | NKSX | WC |
| 59 | **N** | NKSX | WC(S) | | | | | | | | |

### TSO

| | | | | | | | | | | |
|---|---|---|---|---|---|---|---|---|---|---|
| 72 | **N** | NKSX | WC | 77 | **N** | NKSX | WC | 83 | **N** | NKSX | WC |
| 73 | **N** | NKSX | WC | 78 | **N** | NKSX | WC | 84 | **N** | NKSX | WC |
| 74 | **N** | NKSX | WC | 80 | **N** | NKSX | WC | 85 | **N** | NKSX | WC |
| 75 | **N** | NKSX | WC | 81 | **N** | NKSX | WC | 86 | **N** | NKSX | WC |
| 76 | **N** | NKSX | WC | | | | | | | | |

# MERSEYRAIL 750 V d.c. EMUs

## CLASS 507

BDMSO – TSO – DMSO. Tightlock couplers. Sliding doors. Disc and rheostatic brakes. PA.

**System:** 750 V d.c. third rail.
**Bogies:** BX1.
**Gangways:** Gangwayed within unit. End doors.
**Traction Motors:** Four GEC G310AZ of 82.125 kW.
**Dimensions:** 19.80 x 2.82 m (outer cars), 19.92 x 2.82 m (inner cars).
**Maximum Speed:** 75 mph.

**BDMSO.** Dia. EI202. Lot No. 30906 York 1978 – 80. 74S. 37.06 t.
**TSO.** Dia. EH205. Lot No. 30907 York 1978 – 80. 82S. 25.60 t.
**DMSO.** Dia. EA201. Lot No. 30908 York 1978 – 80. 74S. 35.62 t.

| | | | | | |
|---|---|---|---|---|---|
| 507 001 | | RCHR | HR | 64367 71342 64405 |
| 507 002 | | RCHR | HR | 64368 71343 64406 |
| 507 003 | | RCHR | HR | 64369 71344 64407 |
| 507 004 | | RCHR | HR | 64388 71345 64426 |
| 507 005 | | RCHR | HR | 64371 71346 64409 |
| 507 006 | | RCHR | HR | 64372 71347 64410 |
| 507 007 | | RCHR | HR | 64373 71348 64411 |
| 507 008 | | RCHR | HR | 64374 71349 64412 |
| 507 009 | | RCHR | HR | 64375 71350 64413 |
| 507 010 | | RCHR | HR | 64376 71351 64414 |
| 507 011 | | RCHR | HR | 64377 71352 64415 |
| 507 012 | | RCHR | HR | 64378 71353 64416 |
| 507 013 | **MT** | RCHR | HR | 64379 71354 64417 |
| 507 014 | **MT** | RCHR | HR | 64380 71355 64418 |
| 507 015 | | RCHR | HR | 64381 71356 64419 |
| 507 016 | | RCHR | HR | 64382 71357 64420 |
| 507 017 | | RCHR | HR | 64383 71358 64421 |
| 507 018 | | RCHR | HR | 64384 71359 64422 |
| 507 019 | | RCHR | HR | 64385 71360 64423 |
| 507 020 | | RCHR | HR | 64386 71361 64424 |
| 507 021 | **MT** | RCHR | HR | 64387 71362 64425 |
| 507 022 | **MT** | RFXX | HR | 64370 71363 64408 |
| 507 023 | | RCHR | HR | 64389 71364 64427 |
| 507 024 | | RCHR | HR | 64390 71365 64428 |
| 507 025 | | RCHR | HR | 64391 71366 64429 |
| 507 026 | | RCHR | HR | 64392 71367 64430 |
| 507 027 | | RCHR | HR | 64393 71368 64431 |
| 507 028 | | RCHR | HR | 64394 71369 64432 |
| 507 029 | | RCHR | HR | 64395 71370 64433 |
| 507 030 | | RCHR | HR | 64396 71371 64434 |
| 507 031 | | RCHR | HR | 64397 71372 64435 |
| 507 032 | | RCHR | HR | 64398 71373 64436 |
| 507 033 | | RCHR | HR | 64399 71374 64437 |

# CLASS 508

DMSO – TSO – BDMSO. Tightlock couplers. Sliding doors. Disc and rheostatic brakes. PA. Originally built as four car units and numbered 508 001 – 043. One trailer removed and used for class 455/7 on transfer from the SR.

**System:** 750 V d.c. third rail.
**Bogies:** BX1.
**Gangways:** Gangwayed within unit. End doors.
**Traction Motors:** Four GEC G310AZ of 82.125 kW.
**Dimensions:** 19.80 x 2.82 m (outer cars), 19.92 x 2.82 m (inner cars).
**Maximum Speed:** 75 mph.

**64649 – 64687. DMSO.** Dia. EA208. Lot No. 30942 York 1979 – 80. 74S. 36.15 t.
**64688 – 64691. DMSO.** Dia. EA208. Lot No. 30979 York 1980. 74S. 36.15 t.
**71483 – 71520. TSO.** Dia. EH218. Lot No. 30943 York 1979 – 80. 82S. 26.72 t.
**71521 – 71525. TSO.** Dia. EH218. Lot No. 30980 York 1980. 82S. 26.72 t.
**64692 – 64729. BDMSO.** Dia. EI203. Lot No. 30945 York 1979 – 80. 74S. 36.61 t.
**64730 – 64734. BDMSO.** Dia. EI203. Lot No. 30981 York 1980. 74S. 36.61 t.

| | | | | | |
|---|---|---|---|---|---|
| 508 101 | | RCBD | BD | 64649 71483 64692 |
| 508 102 | | RCBD | BD | 64650 71484 64693 |
| 508 103 | **MT** | RCBD | BD | 64651 71485 64694 |
| 508 104 | | RCBD | BD | 64652 71486 64695 |
| 508 105 | | RCBD | BD | 64653 71487 64696 |
| 508 106 | | RCBD | BD | 64654 71488 64697 |
| 508 107 | | RCBD | BD | 64655 71489 64698 |
| 508 108 | | RCBD | BD | 64656 71490 64699 |
| 508 109 | | RCBD | BD | 64657 71491 64700 |
| 508 110 | | RCBD | BD | 64658 71492 64701 |
| 508 111 | | RCBD | BD | 64659 71493 64702 |
| 508 112 | | RCBD | BD | 64660 71494 64703 |
| 508 113 | | RCBD | BD | 64661 71495 64704 |
| 508 114 | **MT** | RCBD | BD | 64662 71496 64705 |
| 508 115 | | RCBD | BD | 64663 71497 64706 |
| 508 116 | | RCBD | BD | 64664 71498 64707 |
| 508 117 | | RCBD | BD | 64665 71499 64708 |
| 508 118 | | RCBD | BD | 64666 71500 64709 |
| 508 119 | | RCBD | BD | 64667 71501 64710 |
| 508 120 | | RCBD | BD | 64668 71502 64711 |
| 508 121 | | RCBD | BD | 64669 71503 64712 |
| 508 122 | | RCBD | BD | 64670 71504 64713 |
| 508 123 | | RCBD | BD | 64671 71505 64714 |
| 508 124 | | RCBD | BD | 64672 71506 64715 |
| 508 125 | | RCBD | BD | 64673 71507 64716 |
| 508 126 | | RCBD | BD | 64674 71508 64717 |
| 508 127 | | RCBD | BD | 64675 71509 64718 |
| 508 128 | | RCBD | BD | 64676 71510 64719 |
| 508 129 | | RCBD | BD | 64677 71511 64720 |
| 508 130 | | RCBD | BD | 64678 71512 64721 |

| 508 131 | RCBD | BD | 64679 71513 64722 |
| 508 132 | RCBD | BD | 64680 71514 64723 |
| 508 133 | RCBD | BD | 64681 71515 64724 |
| 508 134 | RCBD | BD | 64682 71516 64725 |
| 508 135 | RCBD | BD | 64683 71517 64726 |
| 508 136 | RCBD | BD | 64684 71518 64727 |
| 508 137 | RCBD | BD | 64685 71519 64728 |
| 508 138 | RCBD | BD | 64686 71520 64729 |
| 508 139 | RCHR | HR | 64687 71521 64730 |
| 508 140 | RCHR | HR | 64688 71522 64731 |
| 508 141 | RCHR | HR | 64689 71523 64732 |
| 508 142 | RCHR | HR | 64690 71524 64733 |
| 508 143 | RCHR. | HR | 64691 71525 64734 |

# DEPARTMENTAL EMUs

**Individual vehicles.**

| ADB 975032 | (75165) SH | SR class 932 experimental stock. 'Mars'. |
| DB 977335 | (76277) RTC | MTA Pool Generator coach for DB999550. |
| DB 977336 | (76278) Cathays | MTA Pool Driving trailer for DB999550. (pending conversion). |
| ADB 977362 | (10392) BI | SR class 930 deicing trailer. |
| ADB 977363 | (10399) BM | SR Class 930 deicing trailer. |
| ADB 977364 | (10400) RE | SR class 930 deicing trailer. |
| ADB 977578 | (77101) HE | Sandite vehicle. (work with Class 317/319). |
| ADB 977579 | (77109) SU | Sandite vehicle. (work with Class 317/319). |
| DB 999602 | (62483) RTC | Ultrasonic test train instrumentation coach. MTA pool. |
| DB 999603 | (62482) Cathays | Ultrasonic test train coach (pending conversion). |

**Complete Units**

Southern Region Class 930 Deicing and Sandite units.

| 930 003 | SU | ADB | 975594 (12658) | ADB 975595 (10994) |
| 930 004 | EH | ADB | 975586 (10907) | ADB 975587 (10908) |
| 930 005 | WD | ADB | 975588 (10981) | ADB 975589 (10982) |
| 930 006 | WD | ADB | 975590 (10833) | ADB 975591 (10834) |
| 930 007 | GI | ADB | 975592 (10993) | ADB 975593 (12659) |
| 930 008 | AF | ADB | 975596 (10844) | ADB 975597 (10987) |
| 930 009 | BI | ADB | 975598 (10989) | ADB 975599 (10990) |
| 930 010 | BI | ADB | 975600 (10988) | ADB 975601 (10843) |
| 930 011 | RE | ADB | 975602 (10991) | ADB 975603 (10992) |
| 930 012 | BM | ADB | 975604 (10939) | ADB 975605 (10940) |
| 930 013 | RE | ADB | 975896 (11387) | ADB 975897 (11388) |
| 930 015 | WD | ADB | 977531 (14047) | ADB 977532 (14048) |
| 930 016 | AF | ADB | 977533 (14273) | ADB 977534 (14384) |
| 930 017 | EH | ADB | 977566 (65312) | ADB 977567 (65314) |
| 930 030 | AF | | 977804 (65336) | 977805 (65357) |

Southern Region Class 931 Carriage Cleaning Fluid Unit:

| 931 062 | SL | ADB | 977559 (65313) | ADB 977560 (65320) |

Southern Region Class 932 Tractor Units:

| 930 014 | EH | ADB | 977609 (65414) | ADB 977207 (61658) |
| 932 021 | WD | ADB | 977304 (65317) | ADB 977305 (65322) |
| 932 080 | SL | | 977395 (61035) | ADB 977396 (61392) |
| 932 081 | SL | | 977397 (61388) | ADB 977398 (61389) |

Southern Region Test Units:

| 932 050 | SH | ADB | 977296 (65319) | ADB 977297 (77108) |
| 930 053 | SH | ADB | 977505 (65321) | ADB 977507 (77110) |
| 930 054 | SH | ADB | 977506 (65323) | ADB 977508 (77112) |

Class 438 4 TC Unit:

| | | | | | |
|---|---|---|---|---|---|
| 8007 | SL | ADB | 977684 (76282) | ADB 977685 (70818) | |
| | | ADB | 977686 (70850) | ADB 977687 (76281) | |

Anglia Region class 302 three-car Sandite Units:

| | | | | |
|---|---|---|---|---|
| 302 996 | CC | ADB | 977598 (75080) | ADB 977599 (61073) |
| | | ADB | 977600 (75061) | |
| 302 997 | IL | ADB | 977601 (75211) | ADB 977602 (61228) |
| | | ADB | 977603 (75035) | |
| 302 998 | EM | ADB | 977604 (75077) | ADB 977605 (61056) |
| | | ADB | 977606 (75070) | |
| 305 908 | IL | ADB | 977741 (75469) | ADB 977742 (61436) |
| | | ADB | 977743 (75521) | |

Demonstration Unit:

| | | | | |
|---|---|---|---|---|
| 303 999 | IL | ADB | 977711 (75759) | ADB 977712 (61825) |
| | | ADB | 977713 (75815) | |

InterCity Instruction Unit:

| | | | | |
|---|---|---|---|---|
| 305 935 | HA | ADB | 977639 (75548) | ADB 977640 (61463) |
| | | ADB | 977641 (75214) | |

Note: 977641 of 305 935 is a former Class 302 car.

Crash test units (kept at Old Dalby).

| | | | |
|---|---|---|---|
| 307 101 | RTC | 977668 (75001) | 977669 (61001) |
| | | 977670 (70001) | 977671 (75101) |
| 307 106 | RTC | 977672 (75006) | 977673 (61006) |
| | | 977674 (70006) | 977675 (75106) |
| 307 121 | RTC | 977676 (75021) | 977677 (61021) |
| | | 977678 (70021) | 977679 (75121) |

Test unit awaiting conversion.

| | | | |
|---|---|---|---|
| 307 118 | RTC | 977708 (75018) | 977709 (61018) |
| | | 977710 (75118) | |

London Midland Region Sandite Units:

| | | | | |
|---|---|---|---|---|
| 930 501 | SH | ADB | 977385 (61148) | ADB 977386 (75189) |
| 936 001 | BD | ADB | 977345 (61178) | ADB 977346 (75178) |
| 936 002 | BD | ADB | 977347 (61180) | ADB 977348 (75180) |
| 936 003 | BD | ADB | 977349 (61183) | ADB 977350 (75183) |

Note: Most units do not carry '93x' numbers.

## CLASS 419                                   1957 type MLV

DMLV. Built 1959 – 61. Dual braked. These units are now officially in departmental stock, but they retain their capital stock side numbers.

**Electrical Equipment:** 1957-type.
**Bogies:** Mk 3B.
**Gangways:** Non-gangwayed.
**Traction Motors:** Two EE507 of 185 kW.
**Dimensions:** 19.64 x 2.82 m.
**Maximum Speed:** 90 mph.

**68001 – 2. DMLV.** Dia. EX560. Lot No. 30458 Afd./Elh. 1959. 45.5 t.
**68003 – 10. DMLV.** Dia. EX560. Lot No. 30623 Afd./Elh. 1960 – 61. 45.5 t.

| | | | | | |
|---|---|---|---|---|---|
| 931090 | (9000) | J | NBTX | RE | 68010 |
| 931091 | (9001) | N | NBTX | RE | 68001 |
| 931092 | (9002) | N | NBTX | RE | 68002 |
| 931093 | (9003) | N | NBTX | RE | 68003 |
| 931094 | (9004) | N | NBTX | RE | 68004 |
| 931095 | (9005) | N | NBTX | RE | 68005 |
| 931096 | (9006) | J | NBTX | RE | 68006 |
| 931097 | (9007) | N | NBTX | RE | 68007 |
| 931098 | (9008) | N | NBTX | RE | 68008 |
| 931099 | (9009) | N | NBTX | RE | 68009 |

# TRANS-MANCHE SUPER TRAINS

The Trans-Manche Super Trains (TMSTs) are on order for the Channel Tunnel services between London and Paris and Brussels. They are based on the French TGV design concept, and the individual cars are numbered like French TGVs.

Each train consists of two 9-coach sets back-to-back with a power car at the outer end. BR sets will be allocated to North Pole (London), Belgian Railways (SNCB/NMBS) sets will be allocated to Bruxelles Forest/Brussel Vorst and French Railways (SNCF) sets will be allocated to Le Landy (Paris). In addition, there are trains for North of London which consist of two 7-coach half-sets.

All sets are articulated with an extra motor bogie on the coach next to the power car. Coaches are numbered R1–R9 (and in traffic R10–R18 in the second set). Coaches R18–R10 are identical to R1–R9.

**BR Sets.**

| | | | |
|---|---|---|---|
| 3001 | 730010 | 730011 | 730012 |
| 3002 | 730020 | 730021 | 730022 |
| 3003 | 730030 | 730031 | 730032 |
| 3004 | 730040 | 730041 | 730042 |
| 3005 | 730050 | 730051 | 730052 |
| 3006 | 730060 | 730061 | 730062 |
| 3007 | 730070 | 730071 | 730072 |
| 3008 | 730080 | 730081 | 730082 |
| 3009 | 730090 | 730091 | 730092 |
| 3010 | 730100 | 730101 | 730102 |
| 3011 | 730110 | 730111 | 730112 |
| 3012 | 730120 | 730121 | 730122 |
| 3013 | 730130 | 730131 | 730132 |
| 3014 | 730140 | 730141 | 730142 |
| 3015 | 730150 | 730151 | 730152 |
| 3016 | 730160 | 730161 | 730162 |
| 3017 | 730170 | 730171 | 730172 |
| 3018 | 730180 | 730181 | 730182 |
| 3019 | 730190 | 730191 | 730192 |
| 3020 | 730200 | 730201 | '730202 |
| 3021 | 730210 | 730211 | 730212 |
| 3022 | 730220 | 730221 | 730222 |

**SNCB/NMBS Sets.**

| | | | |
|---|---|---|---|
| 3101 | 731010 | 731011 | 731012 |
| 3102 | 731020 | 731021 | 731022 |
| 3103 | 731030 | 731031 | 731032 |
| 3104 | 731040 | 731041 | 731042 |
| 3105 | 731050 | 731051 | 731052 |
| 3106 | 731060 | 731061 | 731062 |
| 3107 | 731070 | 731071 | 731072 |
| 3108 | 731080 | 731081 | 731082 |

**Systems:** 25 kV a.c. overhead, 3000 V d.c. overhead and 750 V d.c. third rail.

**Built:** 1992–3 by GEC Alsthom at various works.
**Wheel Arrangement:** Bo–Bo + Bo–2–2–2–2–2–2–2–2–2.
**Traction Motors:** 6.
**Length:** 22.15 + 21.845 + [7 x 18.70] + 21.845 m.
**Max. Speed:** 300 km/h (187.5 mph).
**Livery:** White with yellow window band.
**Details:**

| Car | Type | Seats | Lot No. | Car | Type | Seats | Lot No. |
|-----|------|-------|---------|-----|------|--------|---------|
| M | DM | | 31118 | R5 | TSOL | 60S 2L | 31123 |
| R1 | MSOL | 52S 1L | 31119 | R6 | Kitchen/bar | | 31124 |
| R2 | TSOL | 60S 1L | 31120 | R7 | TFOL | 39F 1L | 31125 |
| R3 | TSOL | 60S 2L | 31121 | R8 | TFOL | 39F 1L | 31126 |
| R4 | TSOL | 60S 1L | 31122 | R9 | TBFOL | 27F 1L | 31127 |

| | | | | | | |
|---|---|---|---|---|---|---|
| 730013 | 730014 | 730015 | 730016 | 730017 | 730018 | 730019 |
| 730023 | 730024 | 730025 | 730026 | 730027 | 730028 | 730029 |
| 730033 | 730034 | 730035 | 730036 | 730037 | 730038 | 730039 |
| 730043 | 730044 | 730045 | 730046 | 730047 | 730048 | 730049 |
| 730053 | 730054 | 730055 | 730056 | 730057 | 730058 | 730059 |
| 730063 | 730064 | 730065 | 730066 | 730067 | 730068 | 730069 |
| 730073 | 730074 | 730075 | 730076 | 730077 | 730078 | 730079 |
| 730083 | 730084 | 730085 | 730086 | 730087 | 730088 | 730089 |
| 730093 | 730094 | 730095 | 730096 | 730097 | 730098 | 730099 |
| 730103 | 730104 | 730105 | 730106 | 730107 | 730108 | 730109 |
| 730113 | 730114 | 730115 | 730116 | 730117 | 730118 | 730119 |
| 730123 | 730124 | 730125 | 730126 | 730127 | 730128 | 730129 |
| 730133 | 730134 | 730135 | 730136 | 730137 | 730138 | 730139 |
| 730143 | 730144 | 730145 | 730146 | 730147 | 730148 | 730149 |
| 730153 | 730154 | 730155 | 730156 | 730157 | 730158 | 730159 |
| 730163 | 730164 | 730165 | 730166 | 730167 | 730168 | 730169 |
| 730173 | 730174 | 730175 | 730176 | 730177 | 730178 | 730179 |
| 730183 | 730184 | 730185 | 730186 | 730187 | 730188 | 730189 |
| 730193 | 730194 | 730195 | 730196 | 730197 | 730198 | 730199 |
| 730203 | 730204 | 730205 | 730206 | 730207 | 730208 | 730209 |
| 730213 | 730214 | 730215 | 730216 | 730217 | 730218 | 730219 |
| 730223 | 730224 | 730225 | 730226 | 730227 | 730228 | 730229 |

| | | | | | | |
|---|---|---|---|---|---|---|
| 731013 | 731014 | 731015 | 731016 | 731017 | 731018 | 731019 |
| 731023 | 731024 | 731025 | 731026 | 731027 | 731028 | 731029 |
| 731033 | 731034 | 731035 | 731036 | 731037 | 731038 | 731039 |
| 731043 | 731044 | 731045 | 731046 | 731047 | 731048 | 731049 |
| 731053 | 731054 | 731055 | 731056 | 731057 | 731058 | 731059 |
| 731063 | 731064 | 731065 | 731066 | 731067 | 731068 | 731069 |
| 731073 | 731074 | 731075 | 731076 | 731077 | 731078 | 731079 |
| 731083 | 731084 | 731085 | 731086 | 731087 | 731088 | 731089 |

**SNCF Sets.**

| | | | |
|---|---|---|---|
| 3201 | 732010 | 732011 | 732012 |
| 3202 | 732020 | 732021 | 732022 |
| 3203 | 732030 | 732031 | 732032 |
| 3204 | 732040 | 732041 | 732042 |
| 3205 | 732050 | 732051 | 732052 |
| 3206 | 732060 | 732061 | 732062 |
| 3207 | 732070 | 732071 | 732072 |
| 3208 | 732080 | 732081 | 732082 |
| 3209 | 732090 | 732091 | 732092 |
| 3210 | 732100 | 732101 | 732102 |
| 3211 | 732110 | 732111 | 732112 |
| 3212 | 732120 | 732121 | 732122 |
| 3213 | 732130 | 732131 | 732132 |
| 3214 | 732140 | 732141 | 732142 |
| 3215 | 732150 | 732151 | 732152 |
| 3216 | 732160 | 732161 | 732162 |
| 3217 | 732170 | 732171 | 732172 |
| 3218 | 732180 | 732181 | 732182 |
| 3219 | 732190 | 732191 | 732192 |
| 3220 | 732200 | 732201 | 732202 |
| 3221 | 732210 | 732211 | 732212 |
| 3222 | 732220 | 732221 | 732222 |
| 3223 | 732230 | 732231 | 732232 |
| 3224 | 732240 | 732241 | 732242 |
| 3225 | 732250 | 732251 | 732252 |
| 3226 | 732260 | 732261 | 732262 |
| 3227 | 732270 | 732271 | 732272 |
| 3228 | 732280 | 732281 | 732282 |
| 3229 | 732290 | 732291 | 732292 |
| 3230 | 732300 | 732301 | 732302 |
| 3231 | 732310 | 732311 | 732312 |
| 3232 | 732320 | 732321 | 732322 |

**BR "North of London" Sets.**

These are 7-coach sets consisting of PC + R1/3/2/5/6/7/9 only.

| | | | |
|---|---|---|---|
| 3301 | 733010 | 733011 | 733013 |
| 3302 | 733020 | 733021 | 733023 |
| 3303 | 733030 | 733031 | 733033 |
| 3304 | 733040 | 733041 | 733043 |
| 3305 | 733050 | 733051 | 733053 |
| 3306 | 733060 | 733061 | 733063 |
| 3307 | 733070 | 733071 | 733073 |
| 3308 | 733080 | 733081 | 733083 |
| 3309 | 733090 | 733091 | 733093 |
| 3310 | 733100 | 733101 | 733103 |
| 3311 | 733110 | 733111 | 733113 |
| 3312 | 733120 | 733121 | 733123 |
| 3313 | 733130 | 733131 | 733133 |
| 3314 | 733140 | 733141 | 733143 |

| | | | | | | |
|---|---|---|---|---|---|---|
| 732013 | 732014 | 732015 | 732016 | 732017 | 732018 | 732019 |
| 732023 | 732024 | 732025 | 732026 | 732027 | 732028 | 732029 |
| 732033 | 732034 | 732035 | 732036 | 732037 | 732038 | 732039 |
| 732043 | 732044 | 732045 | 732046 | 732047 | 732048 | 732049 |
| 732053 | 732054 | 732055 | 732056 | 732057 | 732058 | 732059 |
| 732063 | 732064 | 732065 | 732066 | 732067 | 732068 | 732069 |
| 732073 | 732074 | 732075 | 732076 | 732077 | 732078 | 732079 |
| 732083 | 732084 | 732085 | 732086 | 732087 | 732088 | 732089 |
| 732093 | 732094 | 732095 | 732096 | 732097 | 732098 | 732099 |
| 732103 | 732104 | 732105 | 732106 | 732107 | 732108 | 732109 |
| 732113 | 732114 | 732115 | 732116 | 732117 | 732118 | 732119 |
| 732123 | 732124 | 732125 | 732126 | 732127 | 732128 | 732129 |
| 732133 | 732134 | 732135 | 732136 | 732137 | 732138 | 732139 |
| 732143 | 732144 | 732145 | 732146 | 732147 | 732148 | 732149 |
| 732153 | 732154 | 732155 | 732156 | 732157 | 732158 | 732159 |
| 732163 | 732164 | 732165 | 732166 | 732167 | 732168 | 732169 |
| 732173 | 732174 | 732175 | 732176 | 732177 | 732178 | 732179 |
| 732183 | 732184 | 732185 | 732186 | 732187 | 732188 | 732189 |
| 732193 | 732194 | 732195 | 732196 | 732197 | 732198 | 732199 |
| 732203 | 732204 | 732205 | 732206 | 732207 | 732208 | 732209 |
| 732213 | 732214 | 732215 | 732216 | 732217 | 732218 | 732219 |
| 732223 | 732224 | 732225 | 732226 | 732227 | 732228 | 732229 |
| 732233 | 732234 | 732235 | 732236 | 732237 | 732238 | 732239 |
| 732243 | 732244 | 732245 | 732246 | 732247 | 732248 | 732249 |
| 732253 | 732254 | 732255 | 732256 | 732257 | 732258 | 732259 |
| 732263 | 732264 | 732265 | 732266 | 732267 | 732268 | 732269 |
| 732273 | 732274 | 732275 | 732276 | 732277 | 732278 | 732279 |
| 732283 | 732284 | 732285 | 732286 | 732287 | 732288 | 732289 |
| 732293 | 732294 | 732295 | 732296 | 732297 | 732298 | 732299 |
| 732303 | 732304 | 732305 | 732306 | 732307 | 732308 | 732309 |
| 732313 | 732314 | 732315 | 732316 | 732317 | 732318 | 732319 |
| 732323 | 732324 | 732325 | 732326 | 732327 | 732328 | 732329 |

| | | | | |
|---|---|---|---|---|
| 733012 | 733015 | 733016 | 733017 | 733019 |
| 733022 | 733025 | 733026 | 733027 | 733029 |
| 733032 | 733035 | 733036 | 733037 | 733039 |
| 733042 | 733045 | 733046 | 733047 | 733049 |
| 733052 | 733055 | 733056 | 733057 | 733059 |
| 733062 | 733065 | 733066 | 733067 | 733069 |
| 733072 | 733075 | 733076 | 733077 | 733079 |
| 733082 | 733085 | 733086 | 733087 | 733089 |
| 733092 | 733095 | 733096 | 733097 | 733099 |
| 733102 | 733105 | 733106 | 733107 | 733109 |
| 733112 | 733115 | 733116 | 733117 | 733119 |
| 733122 | 733125 | 733126 | 733127 | 733129 |
| 733132 | 733135 | 733136 | 733137 | 733139 |
| 733142 | 733145 | 733146 | 733147 | 733149 |

# PLATFORM 5 PUBLISHING LTD.
## MAIL ORDER LIST

| NEW TITLES | Price |
|---|---|
| Motive Power Pocket Book Spring 1993 | 1.80 |
| Coaching Stock Pocket Book 1993 | 1.80 |
| Diesel Unit Pocket Book 1993 | 1.80 |
| Electric Unit Pocket Book 1993 | 1.80 |
| A6 Pocket Book Covers in Blue, Red, Green or Grey | 0.80 |
| British Railways Locomotives & Coaching Stock 1993 **MARCH 93** | 7.25 |
| Light Rail Review 4 | 7.50 |
| German Railways Locomotives & Multiple Units 3rd edition | 12.50 |
| 6203 'Princess Margaret Rose' | 19.95 |
| British Baltic Tanks | 6.95 |
| Exeter-Newton Abbot – A Railway History **SPRING 93** | 25.00 |

**Modern British Railway Titles**

| | |
|---|---|
| Preserved Locomotives of British Railways 7th Edition | 5.50 |
| Departmental Coaching Stock 4th Edition | 4.95 |
| On Track Plant on British Railways 4th Edition | 5.50 |
| North West Rails in Colour | 8.50 |
| The Fifty 50s in Colour | 5.95 |
| British Rail Internal Users (SCTP) | 7.95 |
| British Rail Wagon Fleet – Air Braked Stock (SCTP) | 6.95 |

**Overseas Railways**

| | |
|---|---|
| Swiss Railways/Chemins de Fer Suisses | 9.95 |
| French Railways/Chemins de Fer Français 2nd Edition | 9.95 |
| ÖBB/Austrian Federal Railways 2nd Edition | 6.95 |
| Benelux Locomotives & Coaching Stock 2nd Edition | 6.95 |
| A Guide to Portuguese Railways (Fearless) | 6.95 |
| Railways of Southern Africa Locomotive Guide 1992 (Beyer-Garratt) | 4.00 |

**Other Titles Titles**

| | |
|---|---|
| Midland Railway Portrait | 12.95 |
| Steam Days on BR 1 – The Midland Line in Sheffield | 4.95 |
| Rails along the Sea Wall (Dawlish – Teignmouth Pictorial) | 4.95 |
| The Rolling Rivers | 6.95 |
| The Railways of Winchester | 6.95 |
| British Railways Mark 1 Coaches (Atlantic) | 19.95 |
| Register of Closed Railways 1948 – 91 (Milepost) | 5.95 |
| The Battle for the Settle & Carlisle | 6.95 |
| Rambles by Rail 1 – The Hope Valley Line | 1.95 |
| Rambles by Rail 2 – Liskeard-Looe | 1.95 |
| Light Rail Review 1 (Reprint) | 6.95 |
| Light Rail Review 2 & Light Rail Review 3 | each 7.50 |
| UK Light Rail Systems No.1: Manchester Metrolink | 8.50 |
| Blackpool & Fleetwood By Tram | 7.50 |

Postage: 10% (UK), 20% (Overseas). Minimum 30p.

All these publications are available from shops, bookstalls or direct from: Mail Order Department, Platform 5 Publishing Ltd., Wyvern House, Old Forge Business Park, Sark Road, SHEFFIELD, S2 4HG, ENGLAND. For a full list of titles available by mail order, please send SAE to the above address.

Our giro account number is 65 930 4007.